THE MINDFUL LEADER

THE MINDFUL LEADER

ESSENTIAL SKILLS FOR INSPIRING OTHERS TO GREATNESS

Published 2025 by Gildan Media LLC
aka G&D Media
www.GandDmedia.com

THE MINDFUL LEADER. Copyright © 2025 by Pryor Learning, LLC. All rights reserved.

No part of this book may be used, reproduced or transmitted in any manner whatsoever, by any means (electronic, photocopying, recording, or otherwise), without the prior written permission of the author, except in the case of brief quotations embodied in critical articles and reviews. No liability is assumed with respect to the use of the information contained within. Although every precaution has been taken, the author and publisher assume no liability for errors or omissions. Neither is any liability assumed for damages resulting from the use of the information contained herein.

Front cover design by David Rheinhardt of Pyrographx

Interior design by Meghan Day Healey of Story Horse, LLC

Library of Congress Cataloging-in-Publication Data is available upon request

ISBN: 978-1-7225-0723-7

10 9 8 7 6 5 4 3 2 1

CONTENTS

FOREWORD 7

ONE
Emotional Intelligence and Empathetic Leadership
— 11 —

TWO
Improving Communication Skills
— 37 —

THREE
The Conquest of Procrastination
— 63 —

FOUR
Mastering Negotiation
— 89 —

FIVE
Hiring: A Skill-Based Approach
— 109 —

SIX
How to Keep Your Best Employees
— 135 —

FOREWORD

Pryor Learning has been at the forefront of corporate training, shaping the skills and careers of millions. Founded more than fifty years ago, when Fred Pryor pioneered the "One-day Seminar," Pryor Learning has become one of the nation's leading training providers, offering efficient, affordable, accessible career education for business professionals. Our diverse offerings cater to a wide array of individuals and organizations alike, from small and mid-sized businesses to governments, nonprofits, and Fortune 500 companies.

Offering thousands of in-person seminars offered annually, Pryor Learning is synonymous with practical, hands-on training that delivers results. As the workforce continues to evolve, so do we—embracing new technologies and expanding our reach. Today, we offer a vast array of training options including in-person, live virtual, or on-demand formats, all designed to meet the diverse needs of a constantly changing workforce.

This book, and the series it belongs to, represents the next step in our mission to empower professionals with the essential skills they need to excel. In response to the growing popularity of eBooks and audiobooks, we aim to reach a new generation of learners, equipping them with the tools and knowledge to thrive in their careers. Our goal remains simple: to uphold Fred Pryor's legacy by making high-quality business training accessible to all, regardless of where they are in their career journey.

Join us in a tradition of learning that spans more than fifty years—a tradition that has empowered millions to achieve their professional goals. We invite you to explore the wealth of knowledge contained within these pages, knowing that you are part of something greater—a community dedicated to continuous growth and improvement. Welcome to Pryor Learning, where your success is our mission.

In today's fast-paced and ever-evolving business landscape, leadership requires more than just authority; it demands an understanding of human nature. *The Mindful Leader: Essential Skills for Inspiring Others to Greatness* is a comprehensive resource designed to equip leaders with the tools needed to lead with empathy, clarity, and purpose. Among the many insights, you'll discover the keys to becoming a mindful leader by developing your skills and enhancing your leadership skills to manage, develop, and inspire your employees for optimal success.

This book explores the core of effective leadership, starting with the foundational principles of Emotional Intelligence and Empathetic Leadership, which are critical for building trust and fostering genuine connections. From there, it explores the art of Improving Communication Skills, essential for conveying vision and motivating teams. The journey continues with practical strategies for overcoming one of the most common leadership pitfalls—The Conquest of Procrastination—and moves on to Mastering Negotiation, a vital skill for achieving successful outcomes in any business environment. In a world where mindful leadership values everyone's unique contribution, the chapters on Hiring: A Skills-Based Approach and How to Keep Your Best Employees offer practical strategies for recognizing, attracting, and retaining top talent. By embracing the principles outlined in this book, leaders will not only inspire greatness in others but also cultivate a workplace culture where everyone can thrive.

ONE

Emotional Intelligence and Empathetic Leadership

For anyone in management who oversees or supervises employees, mindful leadership is essential. While it may be tempting to look at what others are doing wrong, mindful leadership is more about self-reflection. Before we can help those we coach or mentor become better leaders, it's best to start with introspection.

In this chapter, we'll start by exploring emotional intelligence and empathetic leadership. Next we'll address how to conquer bad working habits which can get in the way of being a mindful leader. Then we'll discuss how to communicate with appreciation, followed by creating a collaborative work culture. Finally, we'll wrap up with mindfully managing organizational change.

Characteristics of a Mindful Leader

What is a mindful leader? Mindful leadership embodies leadership presence by cultivating *focus*, *clarity*, *creativity*, and *empathy* in the service of others. We want to look very carefully at those four characteristics.

> The four characteristics of mindful leadership: focus, clarity, creativity, and empathy.

Finally, we want to look at the end of that definition: *in the service of others.* Being a mindful leader is very much about serving those we lead. Some people have the mistaken idea that being a leader means bossing people around all day. However, a good leader is someone who helps other people become better.

These four characteristics are the fundamentals of leadership excellence. While some people have a natural inclination toward them, these qualities can be developed and strengthened in anyone. We are all capable of having, expressing, and using these abilities properly. With a little work, we can build up muscles that are weak. Don't fall for thinking, "I'm just not that empathetic," "I can't focus," or "I'm just not creative." Don't let these negative statements become limiting beliefs and prevent you from becoming a mindful leader.

Emotional Intelligence

When talking about mindful leadership, the topic of emotional intelligence always comes up (sometimes abbreviated as EI, or, by analogy with IQ, as EQ). If you attend a lot of self-improvement courses, no doubt you've come across this term.

A leader's emotional intelligence is key to fostering trust, cooperation, and motivation within a team. This creates an environment where others feel heard, supported, and valued. Emotional intelligence is the ability to manage your own emotions and understand the emotions of the people around you.

> Emotional intelligence is the ability to manage your own emotions and understand the emotions of the people around you.

Let's look at the five key elements of emotional intelligence. Daniel Goleman, an American psychologist who popularized this concept in his groundbreaking 1995 book, *Emotional Intelligence: Why It Can Matter More than IQ*, lists five major characteristics of emotional intelligence:

1. Self-awareness
2. Empathy
3. Self-regulation
4. Motivation
5. Social skills

These five characteristics are key to how mindful leaders connect with their teams and navigate challenges. Let's look at these aspects individually and explore how they apply to mindful leadership.

Self-Awareness

Let's start with the first characteristic: self-awareness. Ask yourself, "How can I be a more self-aware and self-regulating leader?" This is not only an important question but the key to becoming self-aware. Here are a few tips for improving self-awareness.

The first tip is to sit with the feeling. For example, the next time you feel angry, try to sit with the feeling before reacting. If you're inclined to immediately jump at everyone who approaches you, ask yourself, "Why am I angry? Why am I feeling this way? What is really going on with me today? Am I reacting to something someone said? Am I upset at an individual? Am I upset at a circumstance? What emotion is informing the other person's behavior? What is causing them to be that way? What is causing me to be so triggered?"

Triggering is a term that is often used today. Some people use it as an excuse: "Oh, I was triggered; that's why I acted that way." But mindful, self-aware leaders don't rely on excuses for their behavior. Instead, they are likely to reflect on the situation and think to themselves, "Why was I triggered? I was triggered because of X. Here's what I can do in the future to be more self-regulating when I feel those emotions coming on."

Being self-aware means understanding your strengths and weaknesses, and knowing when to ask for and offer help.

One more tip for improving self-awareness is to work on communicating openly. Honest, open communication allows you to express your thoughts in a way that provides greater understanding and helps build stronger relationships. Let's look at some ways of communicating openly.

- Make your main points clear.
- Eliminate information that isn't relevant to the other person.
- Listen attentively when someone else is speaking.

> **Tips for Open Communication**
> - Make your main points clear.
> - Eliminate irrelevant information.
> - Listen attentively when someone else is speaking.

Empathy

As you strengthen your self-awareness, the next key characteristic is empathy. Mindful leaders are generally more empathetic and have higher EQs than others. Empathy in leadership means being able to look at someone's behavior and ask yourself, what's really going on here? Maybe their personality or behavior today is not what it usually is. What is really happening with this individual? Mindful leaders ask these questions rather than jumping to conclusions.

By looking beyond surface-level behavior, try to understand what people are communicating nonverbally. For example, if you ask someone to help you on a project and they agree but sound and appear hesitant, recognize that there may be a reason. Maybe they feel overwhelmed or confused but are afraid to say no. It's important to address the hesitancy before moving forward.

Motivation

Another key aspect of emotional intelligence is motivation—both yours and the motivation of others. Let's say it's a matter of your own motivation. By asking yourself some basic questions you may work towards figuring out why you feel that way and lead to improving your motivation. For instance, if you're thinking, "I'm not motivated," ask yourself: "Why did I choose this field or this industry? Why did I choose my current position?"

Some people may respond by saying, "I didn't choose this position. I don't even like this work I do, I was 'voluntold.' They forced me to do this job."

> Ask yourself, why did I choose this field or this industry? Why did I choose my current position?

In reality, no one forced you. Even if they pressured you, you still chose to accept the challenge. Suppose your supervisor says, "I know you normally handle customer service, but I want you to take on payroll also." They either imply or state plainly that your only options are to do payroll, quit, or be terminated. At that moment, you're forced to make a choice. If you choose to handle payroll, then you've chosen that over resigning or being terminated. Even though your options may feel limited, it is still your choice.

Being self-aware and owning your decisions is very important to improving motivation. If you dislike what you're doing and it makes you feel unmotivated, then you may be in the wrong job. You've made the wrong choice for yourself.

Again, ask yourself, why did I choose this field or industry? Why did I choose my current position? These two questions are very important. Don't stop asking the question until you get to the bottom of the feeling that's contributing to your lack of motivation.

Why am I feeling depressed? Why am I feeling anxious? Why do I feel sick to my stomach when I come to work? Why do I feel like I just want to sleep through the day? If you're experiencing these low levels of motivation, don't just think, "I hate my job." It's important to understand why you feel that way. It's time to determine if there's something you can do to change your feeling or the situation, and you may conclude that the best solution is find a new job. Either way, understanding your motivation is key—one of the big key components to becoming a mindful, self-aware leader.

Let's review what we've learned from this chapter so far. Here is a recap:
- Mindful leadership embodies leadership presence by cultivating focus, clarity, creativity, and empathy in the service of others.
- Self-awareness is the first key component of emotional intelligence or EI.
- Communicate openly, make your main points clear, eliminate information that isn't relevant to the other person, and listen attentively when others are speaking.
- Motivation can be improved; it takes work and sometimes hard decisions.

Conquering Bad Working Habits

Let's explore six of the top bad habits that people display in the workplace. Mindful leaders recognize and avoid modeling any of these bad habits: instead modeling good, positive behavior to motivate ourselves and those around them. If we're showing up late or missing deadlines, we're not setting a good example, and are probably compromising both our leadership ability and the respect that we have from others.

> **Six Poor Workplace Habits**
> 1. Showing up late or missing deadlines
> 2. Spending work time on social media
> 3. Displaying negative attitudes
> 4. Procrastination
> 5. Poor communication
> 6. Working long hours

Spending work time on social media is another bad work habit and does not set a good example. It's also a bad work habit to display negative attitudes, and it impairs motivation for those around us. Procrastination—"I'll do it tomorrow, I'll do it tomorrow," and tomorrow never comes—we've all been there, and we all know what a bad habit that is.

Poor communication is another bad workplace habit. Everything goes back to communication, so if we're not good at communicating and don't work hard at building our positive communication muscles, this is a habit we may not be able to get past, simply because we choose not to.

Finally, working long hours sounds like a positive quality. People may say, "She burns the midnight oil; she's such a dedicated employee," but working long hours is a bad work habit.

Let's look a little more into these habits to see what else we can learn.

1. Showing up late or missing deadlines. If you struggle with being on time, the first step is to recognize that you have a problem with time management. It's not somebody else's fault: it's not the traffic, it's not the long red lights that you sit through on your way to work—it's none of that. It all comes down to time management.

Time management is knowing which delays we might encounter and for how long: extra traffic, possible accidents on the freeway, long red lights. It's understanding the risks and managing our time around them.

When we explore the reasons why we're often late or missing deadlines, we can begin to develop solutions. We need to put our time management plan in place. Instead of starting a project at the last minute and cutting that deadline too close or missing it altogether, we need to plan for and start the project earlier. Whatever the target, start early.

Let's look at an example. Maybe you find it hard to get up in the mornings: you're not a morning person, and it's hard for you to wake up. Move your phone (or whatever else you use as an alarm) far away from your bed. This way, when the alarm rings, you're forced to get out of bed to turn it off. You may be irritable when you're forced to get out of bed, but don't lie back down. You're up. Stay up. Force yourself to make these changes and manage your time more carefully.

Another key point: when you're going to be late, communicate immediately and let your team know as early as possible. If you're good about communicating when you're going to be late but find yourself doing that a lot, it will have an unintended but helpful side effect: it may become embarrassing and motivate you to make a change. That in turn will motivate you to make sure that you get out and stay out of bed and you don't linger too long over the morning cup of coffee or do anything else that is likely to hold you up.

2. **Spending work time on social media.** As we already pointed out, this is a terrible example to set. It's easy to get sucked into the cycle of telling yourself, just one more post, just one more video, and before you know it, an hour has gone by that you could have used to finish projects. As a manager, supervisor, or any other type of leader, you may become frustrated or even angry with someone on your team who's spending a lot of time on social media when they should be working. You might say, "When you're spending time on social media when you should be working, you're stealing time from the company." But what if *you're* doing it and setting that bad example for your team? Is it a matter of doing as I say, not as I do? Mindful leaders set the example and avoid spending work time on social media unless it's their job to do so.

One way to manage your time is to track and limit your use of social websites. Instead, set aside time blocks in your day for them. If you have a coffee or lunch break, mark it as a block of time for social media. Avoid logging into social media first thing in the morning, because that may cause you to be late for work, fail to finish a project, or miss a meeting. (Note how these bad work habits can tie into one another.)

If you struggle with sticking to time blocking, consider an app that blocks your social media. It may take some willpower, but it will help. Delete the most tempting apps from your phone, turn off the endless notifications from Instagram, Facebook, or X (Twitter), or leave your phone face down or in a drawer while at work. These tips help keep you from glancing over at every little flicker that comes across the screen.

3. **Negative attitudes.** Negative attitudes are big motivation killers. Self-aware, self-regulating, empathetic, focused, mindful leaders work hard to combat negative attitudes. As leaders, we're not immune and can get caught up in the negativity—we're only human—but it's important to model positivity at work, and there's a good chance it will carry over into our personal life. Or we can do it the other way: we try to be more positive in our personal life, and it carries over to our work life. Either way, we've got to try and display more positivity.

Reflect on what influences your negative attitudes or your bad moods. Go back to the questions discussed earlier. Dig in deep, go inside, and ask, "Why am I feeling this way?" Then take steps to manage the triggers of negative attitudes, behaviors, and comments.

Practice emotional intelligence, going from self-awareness to self-regulation and empathy. Self-awareness: "I am feeling very negative today. I tend to be a pessimistic individual." Maybe you are; maybe you're not an over-the-top cheerleader like your coworker. That's OK. Just become self-aware, and don't blame your attitude on somebody else. Even if you're hardwired to be a little negative or pessimistic, practice self-regulation. You can also have an empathetic approach towards other people who struggle with negative attitudes; that too will make you a more mindful leader.

Don't become defensive when people say things that you don't agree with. Someone with a tenacious negative attitude will jump and snap very quickly when they perceive someone disagrees with them or they disagree with someone else. Negative attitudes promote hypercritical behavior.

There's a difference between the yes-people (the good sort) and the no-people. Yes-people want to hear more about your needs and help you move forward, whereas the no-people will roadblock you, intentionally or not.

Think about it: am I a roadblocker or am I a facilitator? In your interactions with others, listen objectively and think before you respond: "Am I about to say something negative? Even though I'm in a bad mood or I'm a pessimistic person, should I be shooting people down?"

4. **Procrastination.** This may be the mother of all bad work habits. Avoid it by breaking projects into small tasks that you complete in bits. If you can check tasks off your list, even small ones, you'll feel more accomplished. That gives you a good feeling and motivates you to continue. Even the smallest win can make you less inclined to put off tasks.

> Complete the most important or most difficult task of the day first thing in the morning.

Complete the most important or most difficult task of the day first thing in the morning—this is sometimes known as "eating the frog." Act early in the day, early in the week, early in the month, early in the year. Eat that frog.

Try habit stacking: build new, good habits on top of old habits. For example, you may decide, "After I get my coffee every morning, I'll complete the most important task of the day." You're giving yourself a caveat: "I'm going to have coffee first, but then I'm going to do that task." But don't put that off. Don't say, "It took longer to have coffee than I thought," or "Lisa wanted to come up and talk my ear off, and I didn't want to be rude." Those are excuses. Don't give yourself excuses. Jump in and keep the commitments that you make to yourself.

> Don't give yourself excuses.

5. **Poor communication.** As introduced earlier, poor communication is a bad habit in both life and work. One way of improving communication is by seeking clarity when you're unsure. Questions might include, "Tell me what you mean by that again" or "What I'm hearing you say is this: is that correct?" Don't be afraid to ask for an explanation. People appreciate when you repeat back and verify that you understood rather than dreamily nodding and saying, "I get it," and walking away without really understanding what the other person said. Listen actively.

Respond to your emails and messages within a reasonable amount of time—but only during business hours. Now you might say, "I've got to respond to emails around the clock; it's part of my job." Maybe that's the case, and if you don't respond at ten o'clock at night, you're going to get fired. Manage that as best you can.

> When you don't understand something, don't be afraid to ask for clarity.

Remember: barring unforeseen emergencies, you teach people how to treat you. When you allow yourself to be overrun with phone calls, emails, and expectations of immediate responses around the clock, you teach your coworkers that it's OK.

Again, use self-awareness. Evaluate why this is happening: Have I allowed this to happen? Did I even help it happen? Ensure your boundaries regarding communication are firm and that you stick to them.

Another tip is to set a reminder to check notifications once or twice during the workday. If you set boundaries to respond to emails every two hours, use a timer or block time on your calendar to ensure that you stick to it. This prevents email from becoming a constant distraction.

Have a good communication plan, and don't assume that an email is not worth responding to. It may feel that way sometimes, but ignoring messages leads to poor communication.

6. **Working long hours.** While this may sound like a good idea: it means you're a dedicated employee, and you probably are. However just like with communication, setting boundaries between your work life and your personal life is essential. If possible, once the clock hits quitting time, leave emails until the next morning, or set another clear boundary that works for you. Develop a shutdown ritual to help you switch out of the office mode at the end of each day. Consider going into a quiet room and meditating, take a short nap, or do something else to help you switch modes. A mindful leader is a self-regulating leader, and self-regulating includes making sure that your work hours are appropriate.

Let's summarize what we've learned above. We identified six bad work habits. One is chronic tardiness. When we expect to arrive late, it's essential to provide plenty of notice. Always think objectively before responding: stop, think, and then answer. To avoid procrastination, tackle big projects early. A key to positive communication is asking for clarification to avoid misunderstanding what's being communicated. Setting boundaries between work life and personal life is also a key to becoming a more mindful and motivated leader.

Communicating Appreciation

Research suggests that people experience burnout in part because they feel they're not appreciated in the workplace. Whether it's perception or reality, feeling undervalued can significantly contribute to burnout. According to research by Tom Rath and Donald O. Clifton, authors of *How Full Is Your*

Bucket? Positive Strategies for Work and Life, 65 percent of employees reported receiving no recognition or appreciation at all in the previous twelve months. One research firm found that while 80 percent of large corporations have employee recognition programs, only 31 percent of their employees said they felt valued for doing quality work. If 80 percent of large corporations have these programs but less than a third of their employees feel valued, there's a definite disconnect. This points out that the way appreciation is communicated in the workplace isn't working effectively.

Sometimes our efforts at recognizing employees are misguided. Efforts can wind up being a waste of time if the recognition isn't delivered in a way that's meaningful to the person receiving it. This leads to the recipient not feeling appreciated despite our best efforts.

Praise needs to be personal, not general.

Now what does that actually mean? For one thing, praise or recognition needs to be personal. A common mistake that managers make is being too general or impersonal with their praise. Maybe the team as a whole did a great job. You say, "Everybody did a good job," but there were one or two people on that team that really were the driving forces. Consider providing them more personal praise rather than a generic email blast that goes out to everyone. You might say to them individually, "Hey, I saw what you did." You can also acknowledge these outstanding workers before the crowd.

Use the employee's name. Say specifically what they did to make the project a success or make the team's jobs easier.

Look at how a person accepts praise. Try to be specific, and make sure they know you saw them. Today you might hear someone say, "I don't feel seen." Having employees who don't feel seen in the workplace is a big obstacle to motivation. Make your praise as personal as you can and balance it with the specific needs of that individual and how they receive praise best.

Keep in mind that actions may speak louder than words. It's not enough for some employees to hear, "You did a good job." They may feel that compliments are disingenuous or forms of manipulation. For individuals who have heard enough of lip service, actions have more impact. Spend time with them, take them to lunch, help them with a task, talk to them one-on-one. For people like this—which includes many of us—doing is more valuable than telling.

Some years ago, there was a best seller called *The Five Love Languages*. People have different languages for praise as well. Find out their language for praise and appreciation, and then try to meet them where they are. Speak the appreciation language of the recipient.

Say there's a big social event, and you're planning to call an employee in front of everyone, give them an award, and have them make a speech. For some people, a staff appreciation dinner is torture, like going in front of a firing squad. A more introverted individual may rather have a gift card to their favorite bookstore and a personal thank-you. Instead of making a big deal of it, show them through some other type of action that you appreciate them. Find out what their currency is: what do they value? Then pay them, so to speak, in their own currency.

There's another trap that we can fall into when we're giving praise and instruction: saying, "You have done a really good job on this project *except for* . . ." Or giving an employee some sort of affirmation and add, "But if you would only . . ." Basically we've just wiped away all the good that we've done with the initial praise. The individual may only remember the criticism without even hearing the positive part of your message. Do your best to separate praise from criticism.

Separate praise from criticism.

Above all, be genuine with people. Don't be fake. Don't overstate your appreciation. Have you ever met someone who was eager to show you that you were appreciated but was so over-the-top that you shrugged off the praise? You think, "That wasn't real; they're just showing off," or "They don't know how to really talk to me about the things that are important to me as an employee." People want praise to be genuine.

When employees feel truly valued and appreciated, work relationships are less tense. Communication is more positive. Policies and procedures are followed more closely. Staff turnover decreases, and managers report enjoying their work more. Isn't it fun to be a manager of happy people? Maybe you say, "I don't know; I've never been a manager of happy people." It could be that you've had some negative individuals in your group, but it could also be that you haven't been as mindful a leader as you should.

Looking in, being more self-aware, being more empathetic, and following the steps that we've outlined above helps to have happier crews. It also makes it easier for us to be genuine with employees, because now we're all on the same page.

Let's look at what we've talked about in the section above. We should make praise personal, not general. Some employees don't value verbal praise as much as they do actions. Sometimes actions will speak louder than words; sometimes it's a balance of the two. Not everyone is comfortable with public recognition. Know your employees: know what they value, know what they fear. Avoid mixing praise with criticism, because the employee may only hear the criticism. Above all, be genuine. Be real.

Create a Collaborative Work Culture

Research has shown that focused, mindful, and successful leaders are collaborative in their approach to their employees and their teams. Some people think that collaboration means getting a bunch of people together in a room. Sometimes that's true, but more often it's a matter of a meeting of the minds. Furthermore, the group doesn't have to be large. Two people can collaborate.

Many factors play a role in creating the ideal office culture. Few things are more important than building a culture of collaboration. Research from Stanford University reveals that working in a collaborative setting makes employees 50 percent more effective at task completion while also boosting their engagement and motivation. Your team is the lifeblood of your business. The phrase used in human resources—"human capital"—is right. Humans are capital. They are your greatest asset. Building a healthy, collaborative workplace culture is key to positive outcomes for your company. It boosts productivity, engagement, and retention.

A mindful leader sets the tone for collaboration within the organization. In order to be truly collaborative, we need to have a foundation of trust in place. An internally collaborative culture needs a solid foundation of consistent communication and transparency.

Transparency builds trust.

Transparency is one of the biggest trust builders in an organization of any size. Leaders who are open, honest, and transparent, and who communicate, are more trusted by their teams. If they act like the Wizard of Oz—the man behind the curtain—the team feels they're hiding something.

We gain trust by sharing information that everyone needs to do their jobs well. Don't hold anything back. Don't unnecessarily limit access to information. Some people do this as a form of sabotage or ostensible self-preservation. But mindful, self-aware, self-regulating, empathetic leaders are not interested in keeping anything back. They want to fulfill the true definition of a good leader: to make people better. The best way to make people better is to consistently train them and share information. It could simply be a matter of weekly email updates or having regular check-in meetings with the team or individuals. Doing this ensures that everyone is in the mix, everyone's ideas and thoughts are heard, and everyone is seen. When we do these things, we will be trusted.

Sometimes collaboration doesn't seem like the obvious path. Maybe our style is to work more as a self-directed individual. Sometimes a leader thinks, "I would rather work alone. I can get more done," and injects that attitude into the rest of the team, assuming everybody feels that way. This can be a very harmful practice.

Consider designing opportunities for collaboration, for example with cross-functional task forces. Not every job entails a huge project with multiple people from different departments. But when we have the opportunity to work cross-functionally, we should take it.

We may need to take this idea further and create opportunities that encourage working together in a cross-functional team. Departments can become siloed, just working amongst themselves. Explore ways to promote cross-collaboration through a project, training, team building exercise, or cross-functional task force. Even if we only include a few team members from each department, we can use cross-training, having employees shadowing one another, or finding other ways to get them out of their silos so they can see how everybody else works—maybe in a department they don't know a lot about but would love to learn. This can inject new ideas into a company and develop camaraderie between teams.

When we design collaborative experiences for team members and make that part of the regular culture, people learn and grow. They're also more likely to be willing to collaborate on future projects—for example, when it's crunch time and we need all the input from everyone.

Then, of course, there's technology. Your organization may use tools like Slack, Asana, Mural, Microsoft Teams, or Zoom for video conferencing, tracking, and communication solutions; there are many. In any event, look at what you're using in your organization and then ask yourself, is there something better? Are we using it to the full? Maybe we have a Slack or an Asana account, but is anybody really using it? We need to keep those programs going. If we implement them, let's not let them fall by the wayside.

If you need help with platforms that provide rapid development of software to fit tasks that need to be done, but you lack the resources to develop them, consider researching low-code platforms. These tools allow you to create platforms with little to no coding experience required. Businesses are better able to respond to a constantly changing market with collaboration tools that boost their productivity. Ensure people have the necessary tools, know how to use them, and are using them effectively.

Then, of course, evaluate and improve. Once we have any process in place, evaluate it afterwards and identify areas for improvement for next time. Regularly assess your processes in building a culture of collaboration. How did it go this time with this cross-functional design team or that project? What could you do better next time? Collect feedback from your team members. What do they think you can do to improve?

Don't just rely on yourself; ask them. Then review all of the information and feedback and see what you need to revise to make the next collaboration an even bigger success.

In the section above, we learned that building a healthy collaborative workplace culture is key to positive outcomes. Transparency is the key step to building trust. Mindful leaders foster collaboration by designing projects or creating opportunities that require a team of employees. Businesses are better able to respond to constantly changing markets with collaborative tools that boost their productivity, so embrace technology. Regularly assess and approve your processes for building a culture of collaboration. Take the feedback and implement it.

Mindfully Managing Change

Change is inevitable: every organization endures change. Mindfully manage change by taking a people-centered approach to change. When people are involved—as opposed to mere organizations—we can make the change fit the person, as opposed to making the person fit the change.

Look at new techniques and think about different models for managing organizational change. Today organizations are shifting from a focus on outside-in, situation-driven, episodic change to inside-out, employee-driven, continuous change. Called *mindful change management*, this approach requires a new set of skills and competencies. Conduct research to ensure that your change management style incorporates mindfulness characteristics.

Always employ supportive behaviors. As we've already explored, being positive and supportive, especially when facing change, has a huge impact. Being proactive and constructive in our actions and even in our resistance to change is very helpful.

There is such a thing as constructive resistance, and learning more about that and employing it in our change management style may be just the thing that we need to increase collaboration and positive outcomes, while showing that we've been a mindful change management leader.

Of course, positive attitudes go hand in hand with everything we've been saying. Positive attitudes toward change are driven by employees' belief in their ability to manage what is happening around them. Frequently people are averse to change because it's uncertain and they don't know what road it's taking them down. As supportive, mindful leaders with a positive attitude, our goal is to get through some of those barriers and help people embrace change more positively.

Emotional well-being is an important component of managing change. When people are enduring change that they're unsure of and unhappy about, their emotional and mental well-being may suffer. They feel stressed, they feel unsure, rocky, off-kilter. When we do our best as mindful leaders to support emotional and mental processes surrounding change, we can ultimately garner a higher return on our change activities. Research shows that understanding how to navigate emotions in a work setting generates a tangible return on investment, both for individuals and organizations. This goes back to being empathetic, being self-aware, being self-regulated, and being people-centered.

Much of the material discussed above is largely about feeling connected. Mindfulness in leadership is about connecting: empathy, emotional intelligence, self-awareness, self-regulation, motivation, good social skills. These qualities all lead to a more connected organization and assist us in managing change.

It's also important to consider the impact: "What's in it for me?" In change management, let your employees know what's in it for them—why change is going to be good for them. Actually, as younger generations filter through our workplaces, some of the focus is being shifted to what's in it for *us*. Stress how changes have a positive impact on the group as a whole. If you're in an industry where the change that you're implementing may affect the environment, the planet, or society as a whole, let people know that. Help them see not just what's in it for an individual, but what's in it for *us*. This is crucial in managing the new generation coming on board.

In the section above, we learned that we should consider a people-centered approach to change management—what's important to them and what's important in the bigger picture as well. Help them to see not only what's in it for me, but what's in it for *us*. Developing a proactive employee mindset can support positive change behaviors. Encouraging positive attitudes in an individual's ability to deal effectively with change can lead to a higher commitment to the change process. Finally, employers and employees with shared goals and values can manage change more easily. Bottom line: mindful leadership.

Key Points in This Chapter

1. Mindful leadership cultivates *focus, clarity, creativity,* and *empathy* in the service of others.
2. Emotional intelligence (EI, or often EQ) is the ability to manage your own emotions and understand the emotions of the people around you.
3. Five characteristics of emotional intelligence: self-awareness, empathy, self-regulation, motivation, and social skills.
4. Mindful leaders are empathetic and have high EQs.
5. Poor workplace habits: showing up late; missing deadlines; spending work time on social media; negative attitudes; procrastination; poor communication; working long hours.
6. Complete the most important or most difficult task of the day first thing in the morning.
7. Make praise personal, not general.
8. Transparency builds trust.
9. Create opportunities for collaboration.
10. Let your employees know what's in it for them.

TWO

Improving Communication Skills

This chapter is about mastering communication skills with tact and confidence—an extremely important component of mindful leadership. It's broken down into five sections:

1. **Crafting a clear message.** How do you use metaphors to make a point? How do you recover from saying the wrong thing? How do you come back diplomatically?

2. **The unspoken rules of business etiquette.** Of course you want to express your identity, but you need to do it professionally. How do you project an impressive image of yourself? And, especially if you do networking, how do you fit in with virtually any group of businesspeople? No matter what your experience level is, it's important to fit in.

3. **How to give and receive productive criticism and feedback.** We'll discuss how to deal with conflict, betrayals, and angry, negative, or toxic people.

4. **How to read people.** How to read faces and look at various subtle clues to what the person is really saying. We'll also talk about how to remember names, so that when you meet someone a second time, you know at least who they are and what they do for a living.

5. **The dos and don'ts of your workspace.**

Crafting a Clear Message

How do you craft a clear message? At some point in your career, (if you haven't already), you'll be in a meeting with your boss or upper-level management, or maybe you'll be in a job interview. Somebody is going to ask you, "What do you think? What are your thoughts?"

It's important to give your point clearly and concisely without getting wordy; otherwise, your audience is going to lose track, and you're going to lose credibility. One way of crafting a clear message is called the *SEER method*. It's a very simple technique. It stands for:

Summary **E**xpand **E**xample **R**estate

1. **Summary.** Share your opinion in one sentence.
2. **Expand.** Say why you feel this way.
3. **Example.** This is where you add credibility to your point.
4. **Restate.** Repeat the message delivered in your summary.

Let's look at an example of the technique in action. Say your spouse has asked you where you think you should vacation next fall. You answer, "I think we should vacation in the Smoky Mountains. I love it up there." Is that your opinion? Sure it is. Does it have a lot of credibility? Not a lot.

What if I use the SEER method? Summary: "I think we should vacation in the Smoky Mountains." Now the expand and example: "Why do I think this way? It's a great time of year to visit, especially in the fall. For example, the average temperature is 50 degrees and there's some snow up in the mountains." Restate: "Those are some reasons I think we should go to the Smokies."

In real time, it would sound something like this. "I think we should go to the Smoky Mountains next fall. I mean, it's a great time of year to visit. For example, the average temperature is 50 degrees, and there's some snow up in the mountains, and that's one reason I love the Smokies in the fall."

Which one adds more credibility? The first one—"I just like them"—or the second one? Certainly it's the second one.

Now let's talk about something a little more controversial, like politics. Say that you have a neighbor named Richard, and you ask, "Richard, whom are you going to vote for in this year's mayoral election?" Richard says, "I'm going to vote for Mrs. Smith for mayor. I just like her. She's great." Is that Richard's opinion? Sure it is. Does it have a lot of credibility to it? Not really.

What if Richard had used the SEER method? Summary: "I'm going to vote for Mrs. Smith for mayor." Expand and example: "I especially like her stance on a green environment. For example, she has a plan to be 25 percent green in the first two years of office." Or "she has a plan to bring 300 new jobs to the city in the next two years. I especially like her position on bringing high-paying jobs to our area." Restate: "Those are some reasons I'm going to vote for Mrs. Smith."

Which one sounds more credible? "I'm voting for her because I just like her" or the SEER approach? The latter is clearly more credible. Richard explains why he feels this way and gives examples to back it up.

Here is a third example, which you could use in a business situation. Say that you are in a meeting with your boss and another colleague. The purpose of the meeting is to decide which software your company should buy: software A or software B. The other person says, "I think we should purchase software A because it's cheaper by a thousand bucks." You, however, think the company should go with software B.

Whether you're talking to customers, colleagues, your family, or your boss, it's important to find out what is important to the other party. That's how you become persuasive.

In this case, say you work for a call center, and you know that your boss is very motivated by efficiency. She says the software must be easy to use, because the company has some technically challenged employees. Long-term warranties are also important. These are the main selling points.

Here is how the SEER approach would work in this case.

Summary: "I think we should purchase software B." Expand: "Why? It'll save us time when talking to customers." Then you give an example to back up your point: "For example, all the information can be seen using one screen. We don't have to toggle back and forth, saving us time." Circle back around to restate your point: "That's why I think we should buy software B." Then expand again: "Another reason is, it's very easy to use. For example, the manufacturer of software B has a training program that enables all employees to be up and running within four hours. A third reason I like software B is that it offers an extended warranty. It comes with a five-year warranty, which covers all defects. Software A only comes with a two-year warranty."

When using the SEER method, especially in a business situation, state your opinion, expand on why you think so, and then give an example to back up your statement.

If you're on a job interview, you could say, "I think I'm a great candidate for the position." Why? Expand: "I take the initiative at work." Give an example: "I've done this and that." You conclude by saying, "That's why I think I'm a great candidate for this position."

Recovering from Faux Pas

How do you recover from faux pas? When you say or do something you wish you could take back, it's best to backtrack using simple statements:

- I can't believe I just said that; please accept my apology.
- I can't believe I just did that, please accept my apology.
- I shouldn't have said that: please accept my apology.
- That came out wrong. What I meant to say is this . . .
- We all make mistakes, right?
- Not my best moment.

If you happen to say or do something that causes offense, you can say, "I didn't mean to offend you; please accept my apology." And then it's over.

In an email, instead of apologizing, consider, "Thank you for catching that," or "I appreciate you bringing this error to my attention," or "Thanks for flagging this for me." If you're late for a meeting, instead of saying, "Sorry, I'm late," use positive words: "Thanks for waiting for me."

This is what professionals do: they don't make a big deal of faux pas or mistakes. They don't dwell on them; they apologize briefly and move on.

> Don't dwell on faux pas. Apologize briefly and move on.

If someone else makes a mistake, it's best to show some empathy. Again, it's usually best not to make a big deal out of it. Consider expressions of this sort:
- I can see how that could happen.
- Mistakes happen.
- I've made that same mistake myself.
- I'm sure many people have made the same mistake.

These statements offer the other person bridge from where they are now to where they need to be. So those are some quick ideas on how to handle it when other people make mistakes.

To recap what we've covered above: crafting a clear message using the SEER method (summary, expand, example, restate) and how to recover from faux pas.

Unspoken Rules of Business Etiquette

Now we're going to talk about some unspoken rules of business etiquette, which especially apply when you're networking.

Express your identity but do it professionally. How do you project an impressive image of self-confidence, professionalism, and competence? Remember, you've got one chance to make a great first impression.

Let's look at a networking event. The purpose of the networking event is to make business contacts, not to hang out with your friends or coworkers you already know. Approach someone you don't know and introduce yourself. That's why they're there. That's why you're there. Walk up, make eye contact, and keep your shoulders square. Don't turn away. If a handshake is appropriate, use a firm handshake; don't hand them a dead fish. Ask open-ended questions. Introduce yourself: "Hi, I'm Pat, I work at such-and-such a place." When the other person tells you where they work, consider saying, "Tell me about that. What do you like about working there?" This is how business conversations get started.

> Don't interrupt others to talk about yourself.

When you are having a conversation, be careful about autobiographical listening—jumping in and interrupting to talk about yourself. Say you're at a networking event and the other person is talking about what a tough day they've had or how much stress they have at work. When they pause, it doesn't mean they're done. If you jump in and talk about your stressful day or how tough *you* have it at work, you've just cut that person off, even if you're only trying to relate to what is being said. Instead, enter the other person's space: ask open-ended questions. If they talk about what a tough day they're having at work, you can ask, "Tell me about it. What's stressing you out so much?" You're expanding on what they brought up because it's important to them. When they're done, then you can go ahead and say what a tough day you had or how much stress you're under.

If you've ever been subjected to autobiographical listening, you know how disrespectful it feels. It also makes for lost opportunities. When you meet a stranger and ask where they work, rather than jumping in and talking about yourself, ask about their job. Ask what services they use; find out if there are opportunities there.

Ten Tips for Business Etiquette

Here are ten more tips for business etiquette when you are networking with people.

1. **Don't multitask.** This goes beyond putting your phone down. It means being fully present when you're conversing with someone. Don't let your mind drift to think about your boss, your work, or the long drive home. Focus on and engage in the conversation.

> **Ten Tips for Business Etiquette**
> 1. Don't multitask.
> 2. Don't pontificate.
> 3. Ask open-ended questions.
> 4. Go with the flow.
> 5. If you don't know, say so.
> 6. Don't equate your experiences with those of others.
> 7. Don't repeat yourself.
> 8. Stay out of the weeds.
> 9. Listen. Avoid autobiographical listening.
> 10. Be brief. Use the SEER method.

2. **Don't pontificate.** A conversation is a two-way street. If you don't want to listen to the other person or hear another point of view, write a blog. That way nobody can give you their response.

3. **Ask open-ended questions.** Conversations are back and forth: "Tell me about that. Can you give me an example?" That opens up dialogue.

4. **Go with the flow.** While you're conversing, ideas come and go. You need to let this happen. When you hear something that reminds you of an experience you've had, avoid jumping in with a story that has nothing to do with the conversation. Stay on topic.

5. **If you don't know, say you don't.** There's nothing wrong with saying, "I don't have that experience," or "I don't know the answer."

6. **Don't equate your experiences with those of others.** This is a networking no-no. It's a lot like autobiographical listening. If the other person's talking about the stress they have at work, don't jump in and talk about how much you hate your boss. It's not the same; it's never the same.

7. **Don't repeat yourself.** Say it once, use the SEER method, and move on.

8. **Stay out of the weeds.** Don't get bogged down with every single detail, because the details usually aren't that important. The other person wants to hear about you but usually only in a broad scope.

9. **Listen.** We all know about listening skills. Again, avoid autobiographical listening.

10. **Be brief. Use the SEER method** to make your point.

Expressing a Professional Identity

How do you express your identity professionally? How do you project an image of self-confidence, giving the impression that you are professional and that the other person should be talking to you? Here are some tips:

When you're standing during a conversation, maintain good posture: stand tall and avoid slouching, which can give the appearance that you don't care. Keep hands and arms open. Openness conveys receptiveness to the conversation. Position your shoulders squarely towards the other person to further express your engagement in the conversation.

As for eye contact, you don't have to stare somebody down, but make an effort to maintain eye contact. If this is tough for you, look at the person's forehead for a couple of seconds, shift to their chin, then come back and look at their cheek. This way, you appear to make eye contact. Finally, smile. Have some fun; be pleasant and smile.

Keep your clothes looking freshly pressed. There is nothing worse than going to a professional event and seeing someone in nice clothes that are wrinkled. Put effort into your appearance—and make it show. Showing up with a wrinkled shirt, blouse, or pants, gives the impression that you don't care.

Pay attention to your nails. Manicure them; clip them. Fastidious nails indicate that you're likely to pay attention to details at work. It's the little things that make a big difference.

Invest in the best shoes you can afford, not only for comfort reasons but also for a professional appearance. Wearing a great-looking outfit with ratty shoes can create a negative impression. Keep your shoes polished and scuff-free. If the heels are worn down, have them repaired. Another quick tip: buy cedar shoe trees. They preserve the shape of your shoes, but they also absorb moisture and control odor.

Pay attention to your accessories. Invest in some high-quality, useful accessories. If you use a briefcase or portfolio, you don't need to spend a lot, but use one that conveys a professional image. If you have them, carry business cards and carry a pen, especially if you're networking. When you meet someone for the first time, they may hand you their business card. When the conversation breaks, you can write a couple of notes down on the back of their card: the person does this at the company, or you should make a follow-up call. If you don't have a pen, you're won't be able to make those notes.

Always keep a jacket or some other item of business attire handy. Consider keeping it in your office or your car. Protect it with a garment bag. You never know when you'll get a last-minute call to meet with a client or customer. It never hurts to be prepared.

Avoid clothing that doesn't look good because it's too tight, too short, too baggy, too revealing, or has holes. If you're not sure whether you should wear an item of attire, don't take the chance, especially in a business situation.

Another quick tip: bring an extra tie, dress shirt, or blouse to a networking or business meeting. You never know when you're might spill a bit of coffee or get ketchup on your shirt or tie.

Here are a couple of other ideas for communicating in a professional manner. Instead of saying, "Sorry to interrupt you," you might say, "I'd like to add . . ." or "I have an idea," or "I'd like to expand on that." When making a complaint, instead of saying, "Sorry to complain," consider saying, "Thank you for listening." This creates a much more professional image and creates a positive tone when you bring up a different point of view.

* * *

We've talked about business etiquette, how to express your identity professionally, and how to fit into virtually any group of businesspeople, no matter what you have in common.

Productive Criticism and Feedback

Next, we'll cover giving and receiving productive criticism and feedback, and how to manage angry people, conflict, betrayal, toxic personalities, and negativity in a professional environment.

When giving feedback to a coworker or employee, do so in private, never in public. Calling them out in public may cause embarrassment and may lead to more disruptive behavior.

The key to giving productive feedback is to attack the problem, not the person. Avoid saying, "You did this." Instead, talk about the problem and not the person. Avoid saying things like, "Steve, you are killing this team because you can't hit the deadline." That's personal. Instead, you might say, "When these deadlines are not met, this is how it affects our production schedule." Talk about the problem—the deadlines—rather than saying "you" in an accusatory fashion.

> When giving feedback, either positive or corrective, use examples.

When giving feedback, either positive or corrective, use examples. Examples of unwanted behavior adds credibility to the feedback. It should also be timely. Don't wait five months before providing feedback; by then it has lost its focus and is not as meaningful. Waiting an extended time to share feedback also creates a situation where the individual receiving the feedback may be unaware of an issue and is unable to make a positive change.

Finally, focus on the future, not the past. Many people and companies spend 90 percent of the time talking about the problem—whose fault it is, blaming people—and only 10 percent of the time looking for solutions. Mindful leaders flip the numbers around: they spend 10 percent of the time talking about the problem, 90 percent of the time looking for solutions.

On the flipside, if you're the one receiving the feedback, and if the individual you're dealing with is angry, don't lose your cool. Do your best to stay focused and maintain control. Imagine this scenario, you have a supervisor stomping towards you, ranting about the month-end figures you gave them yesterday, claiming they're inaccurate. The supervisor attacks you personally by saying, "Listen, if you don't start shaping up quick, you might as well look for another job," or "A two-year-old would spot this mistake you're making."

Rather than panicking and saying, "I'll do better," you can turn this into a more productive interaction by taking a breath and responding: "I want to correct the problem. What specifically is wrong with my report?" Be calm and act in a professional way. It may not be a matter of the entire report: the boss may just have a problem with a very small part of it.

When receiving feedback, listen before you speak. Seek first to understand and then to be understood. Ask questions and ask for examples: "What do you mean by this?" When you don't agree with the feedback, listen for the facts. Ask yourself, is there any possibility that this could be accurate—at least some of it? Consider talking to a coworker for another perspective: "My boss told me that I sometimes do this; have you ever noticed that?" Again, it's a matter of moving forward, going back to the 10/90 rule: 10 percent problem, 90 percent solution.

Don't buy into the negativity of toxic people.

When you are dealing with anger, conflict, or toxic personalities in the workplace, remain professional. Don't buy into their negativity. Mindful leaders manage the gap between the stimulus and the response. How long does it take the limbic system (which governs our emotional reactions) to come up with a response? It's less than a second. Something happens that irks us, and we're ready to fire off our response. If you've ever said anything you wish you could take back, you know what this is about.

It's better to respond rather than react. A reaction is driven by emotion. A response is driven by rational thought. Respond by asking questions: "Give me an example. What do you mean by this?" Then give your response calmly and professionally.

> A reaction is driven by emotion.
> A response is driven by rational thought.

When there is a problem at work, solve the problem first and deal with the emotions later. Some people get so caught up in emotions—how much they hate something and how much it bothers them—that they never even address the problem. Solve the problem first; deal with the emotions later.

Both in a professional environment and in your regular life, it's valuable to put things in perspective. Try the time warp game. When you're feeling stressed or you're under a lot of pressure, ask yourself, "One year from now, is it really going to matter?"

You'll find that many of the things that upset you today won't matter a year from now—or for that matter a week from now.

When you experience conflict with your boss or a colleague, it is important to establish common ground. What do you both agree about? How do you want this conversation to end? We both want this outcome; how do we get there? This is usually where the conflict lies.

Be prepared to deal with people who are aggressive, loud, overbearing, and confrontational, because you're never going to change them. Speak quietly and firmly. Again, think about common ground. What do you want to accomplish when you communicate with this person? Avoid confrontation, especially in front of other people. Demonstrate that you value the person's experience and passion: "I respect the fact that you have a lot of experience in this matter. I respect the fact that you have a very strong opinion about this." This helps establish common ground and brings defenses down, creating a more open and productive dialogue.

When dealing with an angry person who is passing blame, use scripts like, "I'm here to find a solution, not to place blame." "I'm not going to go into the blame game." "Let's fix the problem instead of finding the blame."

Additional scripts to consider include, "Would you be open to hearing some more ideas?" or "Can I tell you what I think about this?" or "Maybe can we synergize on this?" When they say, "OK," that gives you a chance to express your thoughts.

What's the best way to deal with a Negative Ned or Negative Nellie. No doubt there will always be people like that in working environments. Avoid getting involved in their negativity. Don't add fuel to the fire by saying, "Yep, yep, yep," even though you disagree. Holding people accountable is important. If the negative person is talking about the boss, Mr. Smith, consider asking, "Have you talked to Mr. Smith about this?" If the answer is no, you have your response: "I would prefer not to hear about it until you've talked to Mr. Smith." This response is not confrontational, you're simply saying that you don't need to be hearing this: "I don't want to hear the gossip about the boss until you've actually addressed it with him or her."

The Art of Remembering Names

Has this ever happened to you? You just met a business contact, you've exchanged names, and five seconds later, you've totally forgotten their name. Or how about this? You meet someone at a business function, and you talk for quite a while, and you don't see them again for several months. Then one day you run into them at some unusual place, like the bank or the grocery store, and they remember your name. They ask questions about your family and your business. You have no idea who they are, but they look familiar. How do you handle situations like this?

Remembering names and information about people is not about memorization; it's about recall. If you hear the information, it's stored in your brain. But can you recall it when you need to?

Here are some simple steps for recalling facts, data, information, and, of course, names.

In the first place, avoid thinking, "I'm just bad with names." That's an excuse that you don't even want to try to remember someone's name. Instead, use a positive approach: "I'm great with names. I will remember this person's name." When you meet somebody new, say to yourself, "I'm going to remember their name." It's amazing how that positive attitude goes such a long way in helping remember people's names.

Catch the name the first time.

The next step: catch the name the first time. When you meet someone, get everything else out of your mind for the first few seconds, because their name is coming. Don't be thinking about what you're wearing or what you're going to say. Catch their name. If you don't catch their name for whatever reason, ask for it again right away. You don't want to be introducing yourself to someone and then find yourself thinking for five minutes, "I hope somebody mentions their name." Don't do it. It's very uncomfortable. Just do it right away: "I'm sorry, can you tell me your name again?"

Use this memory trick to help remember someone's name. Use visualization to make the name stick in your mind. Visualization goes a long way when you're trying to remember information. It's easier to remember someone's name when you visualize something that you can attach the name to.

Let's look at some examples. Say you met Mr. Hardy. You might associate him with the fast-food chain Hardee's. You might connect him with Laurel and Hardy and picture him walking around like Oliver Hardy. Whatever works for you—the crazier, the better. Say you meet somebody whose name is Ray. You might picture him with Ray-Ban sunglasses, maybe with a ray of sunshine beaming down on him.

How about Carol? You can picture her singing Christmas carols in a choir. You can picture her tugging her ear: in the old *Carol Burnett Show* on TV, she would tug her ear at the end as a way of saying hello to her grandmother. The crazier you can make it, the better.

Use memory tricks to remember names.

Associations and visualizations are extremely important. While you may not remember the name, you may remember the sun beaming down on that man wearing sunglasses or that woman singing a carol.

How about something a little tougher? How about a name like Mr. Janowski, a name that doesn't automatically conjure a visual image for association. Consider breaking the name down into smaller chunks. For example, you might picture a *janitor* riding a *cow* on a pair of *skis*: Jan-Cow-Ski. If you remember part of it, it'll get you to the last part. With longer and tougher names, you may need a couple of different images.

This happens quite frequently. You're at a business function, and someone introduces you to their coworkers, saying, "This is Mary, Susan, Steve, Mike, Tim, and Mark." You don't have time to make a word association to transfer the name from short-term to long-term memory.

Here's a suggestion. Say your acquaintance is introducing you to five or six of their coworkers. As soon as they say the person's name, jump in, be assertive, move forward, maybe put your hand out, and make eye contact: "Hi, Mark, I'm Pat. Nice to meet you." Here's the second person, Susan: "Hi, Susan, nice to meet you also." Here's the third person—eye contact, handshake. "Hi, Mary, it's nice to meet you."

This way, you slow the introductions down. You have the time to fix a visual image of the person you're meeting and make an association. If you're being introduced to five people and you can remember three of the names, it's a start.

How do you introduce someone when you can't remember their name? Say you're at a business function, and you're talking to one of your colleagues. Someone comes walking towards you and addresses you by name. You're thinking, "Who is this person? What am I going to do now?" You're going to have to introduce them to your colleague and you can't remember their name, but they remember yours. It's a very embarrassing situation.

What can you do? You simply don't introduce anybody. Hopefully that'd be a short conversation, but it's probably not going to happen.

Here's something that works quite often—not always, but often. You're talking to your colleague. Here comes a person whose name you don't remember. When they're walking towards you, greet them with some enthusiasm. You might shake their hand and say, "Hey, it's good to see you again. Have you had a chance to meet my colleague, Mary?" Slightly guide their hand towards your colleague and step back a little. There's a good chance that they're going to step up and say, "No, I haven't. My name is such and such." Now you're out of it.

Typically people introduce the person they know first, and then they're stuck with person number two, whose name they don't remember. Here you start with the person you *don't* know: "Hey, it's good to see you; have you had a chance to meet my colleague, Mary?" If it works 50 percent of the time, that's not a bad batting average.

Reading Postures and Stances

Here are some subtle nonverbal clues about reading postures and stances. Low-power poses include standing with legs crossed, hiding hands. When sitting and looking away or down, with crossed arms and legs, it creates a negative impression. The same can be true of leaning forward, looking dejected. Some people cross their arms simply because they're comfortable or maybe they're cold, but this can be interpreted as defensiveness: being closed off. Make a conscious effort to keep your arms relaxed and open, with your hands also open.

Think about going to a job interview. Many companies ask for feedback from the receptionist about the potential job candidate. While sitting in the lobby's waiting room, the receptionist may be watching and gauging the applicant. If this is you as the job candidate, think about how you may come across. What do you look like when you sit? Do you appear bored? Do you give the impression that you're just going through the motions? Are you excited to be there? When you're in a public forum like this, people are watching all the time—or it's safe to assume they may be watching you.

Power poses: These convey confidence with open hands, looking and leaning slightly forward. Or you may have observed this by seeing someone standing, with hands on their hips and a wider stance as opposed to crossed legs.

Other subtle gestures to look for: relaxed shoulders, eye contact, a slight smile. Steepling your hands: that is, holding your hands apart but with your fingertips touching—like a church steeple. This often indicates that we're coming together on our thoughts, we're connecting, we're moving in the right direction. It is generally a sign of confidence.

Additional nonverbal clues you may notice: Say you're presenting an idea to someone. They give you the right answers: "Oh, yeah, I understand." But if they squint their eyes a little, pushing their nose up, the person may be conveying the nonverbal message, "I'm trying hard to see this, but I just don't understand." When people tilt their head slightly, they're trying to look at the situation from a different angle: that is a sign of confusion. If you see squinted eyes or a head tilt when you are making an important point, you might want to back up and make your point again.

Here's a subtle gesture that you can see in audiences at live events. When somebody is tugging their ear or grabbing their eyeglasses, it often means they want to ask a question; they want to participate in the discussion. That goes back to childhood days. When we were kids in school, what were we taught to do when we had a question? We were taught to raise our hand. Adults have never really gotten out of that habit, but they're much better at hiding it. They'll make subtler, somewhat stifled gestures such as grabbing at their ear or eyeglasses. This means, "I should be raising my hand, but I don't want to do it all the way." When you see gestures like these, you may want to back up and let the other person participate and ask the question they might have.

Do's and Don'ts of the Workspace

Now let's turn to some of the dos and don'ts of workspace decor. When decorating your company office space, follow company policies about what you can and can't have in your workspace. Always follow company policies.

If you're working at home, use common sense. Don't display anything that could be seen as offensive or cause conflict. That might be a calendar with pictures that some people might consider to be offensive, or any political material. That person may be your candidate, but other people may not see it your way.

In a physical office, be very careful if you choose to use air fresheners, especially if coworkers are nearby or you're in an open workspace. You may have great intentions, but you may offend someone who has allergies. Avoid listening to music, videos, or podcasts aloud; wear earphones.

Avoid keeping sweets or candy at your desk, especially if you're trying to eat healthy or you don't want a lot of drop-by visitors. When you have great candy on your desk, coworkers want to come by to get some of it, and they stay to chat.

Here are some dos for decorating your office space. Decorate your workspace with things that make you feel comfortable: plants, memorabilia, trophies, awards, books, even motivational posters. Include personal items such as photos of family, fishing trips, or vacations. Things like these make you feel good. When you're tired or work is stressful, you can look at those photos and say, "Hey, this is what's important in my life. This is why I go to work every day."

Finally—and this is very important—invest in a good chair with great support. If you're sitting for long periods of time when you work, you must invest in a good chair, especially one that is adjustable and has solid lumbar support. You can skimp on other things, but a good chair is like a pair of good shoes: you're going to use them all day, every day.

Key Points in This Chapter

1. Craft a clear message. Use the SEER method.
2. Don't dwell on faux pas. Apologize briefly and move on.
3. Observe the unspoken rules of business etiquette.
4. Don't interrupt others to talk about yourself.
5. Give productive criticism and feedback.
6. Don't buy into the negativity of toxic people.
7. Respond instead of reacting.
8. Learn how to read people.
9. Use visualization to remember names.
10. Learn the dos and don'ts of workplace decor.

THREE

The Conquest of Procrastination

Procrastination is a complex phenomenon. It is influenced by various cognitive, emotional, and behavioral factors. It's the result of the interaction of various brain regions and systems. Some research suggests that procrastination may be related to how the brain regulates and manages tasks and goals. Certain brain areas and systems, such as the prefrontal cortex and the amygdala, may play a role in this process. Other factors, such as impulsivity, emotional regulation, and decision-making, may also contribute to procrastination.

Causes of Procrastination

Ultimately, the exact causes of procrastination are not fully understood, and more research is needed to fully appreciate the underlying mechanisms. But that doesn't mean all is lost. There are many strategies, techniques, and tips that will help you to overcome procrastination, even if we don't totally understand it.

People tend to procrastinate and lose focus in the workplace for a variety of reasons. Here are some of the more common ones.

The first is lack of motivation or interest in the task at hand. This can contribute to procrastination in several ways. For example, if you are not motivated to complete a task, you may find it difficult to start it or maintain focus and concentration on it. Similarly, if you are not interested in a task and you perceive it as unimportant or unengaging, you may be less likely to invest time and effort into completing it. You may be more likely to engage in other activities that are more pleasurable or rewarding, leading to further procrastination.

Difficulty or perceived difficulty of a task also contributes to procrastination in several ways. If you perceive a task as difficult, you may be more likely to put it off or avoid it altogether. This is because difficulty can increase feelings of anxiety and uncertainty, which makes it more challenging for you to initiate or engage in that task. In such situations, you may feel overwhelmed by the perceived challenge, which further intensifies procrastination. You may even lack the necessary skills or knowledge to complete the task. Research suggests that when a task is difficult, it requires more cognitive resources, which may lead to mental fatigue and procrastination.

Distractions such as social media or other leisure activities provide an unfortunately easy and available alternative to the task at hand. When you're faced with the task, you may find it easier to engage in other activities, such as checking social media or watching videos. They provide an instant gratification that can be particularly appealing (because they're often designed to be engaging and enjoyable), but which can make it difficult for you to resist the temptation to engage in them and focus on your long- or short-term goals: you're battling between the quick fix on social media and getting the work done. These activities can take away a great deal of time and energy from completing tasks. If you get reports on your smartphone of how much screen time you've had, sometimes it can be a little shocking to realize how much you have gotten caught in the social media whirl.

The next common reason for procrastination is feeling overwhelmed or too many tasks on your to-do list. In this situation, it is hard to focus on any one for a prolonged period of time. You may find it difficult to prioritize and organize tasks, to the point where you don't even know where to start. Having too many tasks feels overwhelming, which causes you to feel stressed and anxious, leading to further avoidance. You can even fall into a cycle of procrastination where you keep postponing tasks till the next day, which increases the number of tasks you must do, making you feel still more overwhelmed.

Poor time management can lead to a last-minute rush.

Next is poor time management, which contributes to procrastination in several ways. When you don't manage your time effectively, you may not have enough time to complete all your tasks, which can lead to feelings of stress and anxiety. This can make it difficult for you to start or engage in any of the tasks. Poor time management also leads to a last-minute rush: you are trying to complete your work at the last moment, which can often lead to lower quality of work and can definitely lead to stress. Underestimating the time required to complete tasks generates frustration and procrastination when you realize you've run out of time altogether. If you don't manage your time well, you might also find that you have blocks of time with nothing scheduled, which you may fill with leisure activities, social media, or distractions instead of the task at hand. The good news is that time management is a skill that can be learned.

> Time management is a skill that can be learned.

A lack of clear goals or direction can contribute to procrastination by making it difficult for you to understand the purpose or the importance of a task. When you don't have clear goals or direction, it can be hard to know what you should be working on. This can lead to lack of focus and motivation (which was the first common reason for procrastination). In this situation, you may find it difficult to set priorities. A lack of clear goals or direction can in turn make it hard to measure progress or success—another obstacle to motivation and engagement. You may also feel a sense of aimlessness and lack of direction. It can be hard to identify what is truly important in your work, which can lead to procrastination and lack of productivity.

Procrastination and lack of focus can be caused by a combination of these factors, and they can be intensified by stress, anxiety, and other mental health issues. Understanding the underlying causes of your procrastination can help you develop strategies to overcome it and improve your focus.

Overcoming Procrastination

Now let's discover how to conquer the common causes of procrastination. Here are some effective strategies:

- Develop a clear understanding of what you want to accomplish and set specific measurable goals to work towards.
- Break down complex tasks into smaller, manageable chunks.
- Once you've broken down your tasks in this way, prioritize them based on importance and urgency; then set a deadline for each step or task.
- Use time management techniques to plan your day, week, and month in advance.
- Use a calendar or a to-do list to help you stay on track and manage your time effectively.
- Identify and eliminate sources of distraction, such as social media or other leisure activities, that are preventing you from focusing on your work. Tactics could include turning off your phone, closing unnecessary tabs on your computer, or finding a quiet place to work.
- Reward yourself for completing tasks with small treats or breaks. This will keep you motivated (eliminating

a primary cause of procrastination) and will make it easier for you to focus on your work.

The Role of Fear

There is another common reason for procrastination, and it is a big one—fear. There are at least four common fears in the workplace that affect mental endurance.

1. **Fear of failure.** This is a powerful fear that holds people back and prevents them from taking necessary risks or pursuing new opportunities.

2. **Fear of change.** The fear of change leads to resistance and difficulty adapting to new situations.

3. **Fear of the unknown.** The unknown can be scary, making it difficult to embrace new challenges or take on new roles.

4. **Fear of conflict.** The fourth and final fear is the fear of conflict. Although conflict is a natural part of any workplace, some people are afraid of confrontation or disagreement, which affects their mental endurance and their ability to work effectively with others.

Now let's learn how to overcome the four common fears.

1. **Fear of failure.** Setting unrealistic or overly ambitious goals, increases the chance for failure. Setting realistic goals

> **Four Common Fears**
> 1. Fear of failure
> 2. Fear of change
> 3. Fear of the unknown
> 4. Fear of conflict

increases the likelihood of success, which can help build confidence and reduce the fear of failure. Confidence has an inverse relationship with the fear of failure. If you have confidence, you're more likely to eliminate the fear of failure.

Large tasks can be overwhelming. To mitigate this problem, break them down into smaller, more manageable steps. This will make the tasks seem less daunting and increase the chance of success.

Recognize and celebrate small successes. This is a little thing that can be done to build momentum and maintain a positive attitude, reducing the fear of failure and increasing motivation.

Mindful leaders recognize that failure provides valuable feedback. When we experience failure, it's the perfect time to understand what went wrong and what can be done differently. How can you avoid similar mistakes in the future? Failure can be seen as a gift when you get past the fear of it.

2. **Fear of change.** Change brings new opportunities and positive outcomes. Try to focus on the potential benefits of the change and how it can improve your life and work. Change

can be overwhelming, especially if it's a big one. To make the change less daunting, try breaking it down into smaller and more manageable steps. This will make the change seem less overwhelming and increase the chance of success.

Being able to adapt to change is an important life skill. When change happens, be open to the new possibilities and go with the flow. One of the best ways to overcome the fear of change is to take action. Start small and take the first step in the direction of the change. Once you get started and begin to build momentum, accepting the change becomes easier.

3. **Fear of the unknown.** This often stems from a lack of information. Gather as much information as possible about the unknown situation. Doing this helps reduce uncertainty and increase your sense of control. The unknown can be overwhelming, but it's important to remember that you can't control everything. Identify what you can control and focus on taking action in those areas. The unknown is a part of life, and you can't always control what happens. Try to embrace uncertainty and see it as an opportunity for growth and learning.

The unknown can be intimidating. Again, taking small steps towards the change helps you build momentum and make the unknown seem less daunting.

Overcoming fear of change and the unknown is really about seeing the opportunities and possibilities rather than the negatives. It's a little bit of a mind shift.

4. **Fear of conflict.** One key to resolving conflict is effective communication. Communication is a key component that we addressed earlier, and it comes up again as we talk about conflict. Focusing on active listening which involves paying close attention to what the other person is saying without interrupting and without getting defensive can reduce misunderstanding and build trust. It's easy to become entrenched in your own point of view, but trying to understand where the other person is coming from can help you to reduce conflict. For more about this concept, see *The Seven Habits of Highly Effective People,* by Stephen R. Covey. The fifth habit addresses seeking to understand versus being understood: focusing on understanding the other person versus getting them to understand you.

Assertive communication involves expressing your thoughts and feelings in a clear and direct way without being either aggressive or passive. This stance can reduce the likelihood of misunderstandings while setting clear boundaries.

If you've contributed to the conflict, take responsibility. If an apology is necessary, give one. This way, you can diffuse a situation and move towards resolution.

Finally, conflicts often arise when people have different needs or wants. Practice compromise. Find a middle ground and reach a resolution that satisfies both parties. You're looking for areas that you and the other party have in common. If you ask why and can find commonality in what you want and why you want it you have an opportunity to find a compromise solution.

Three More Strategies

There are three more strategies for conquering the common causes of procrastination and overcoming the four fears that impact mental endurance and productivity.

1. **Embrace a growth mindset.** Mindful leaders take on a growth mindset and believe that they can develop their abilities through effort and learning. Embracing this mentality refocuses failure as an opportunity to learn and grow rather than as a setback. It can also help you view change as an opportunity to learn and grow rather than as a threat. A growth mindset is also helpful as you implement the strategies and techniques you are learning to conquer procrastination once and for all. If you want to learn more about the growth mindset, you can check out the book *Mindset: The New Psychology of Success* by Carol Dweck.

> Embrace a growth mindset.

2. **Practice mindfulness.** Mindfulness allows you to stay present and focused in the moment rather than getting caught up in worrying about the future or what others may be thinking. Techniques like meditation and deep breathing can be used to manage stress and anxiety associated with the fear of change and the unknown. Focusing on the present moment allows you to be more engaged and less self-conscious. These tech-

niques can also help you manage your emotions amid conflict, enabling you to remain calm and rational. Mindfulness can also promote a growth mindset and reframe how you view failure by recognizing opportunities to learn and grow.

3. Seek support. Surround yourself with supportive people who encourage you to take risks and celebrate your successes. Also, don't be afraid to seek guidance from a therapist or counselor to work through underlying issues that may be contributing to your fear of failure. If your fear of conflict or of being judged is affecting your daily life, therapy can develop coping strategies to manage these fears. Change can be difficult, and it's important to have a support system in place. Seek out the support of friends and family, who can provide guidance and encouragement when you're facing change.

> Surround yourself with supportive people.

Above, we discussed strategies to conquer the common reasons for procrastination, loss of focus, and lack of mental endurance. We've also discussed techniques for overcoming four main fears, including these three strategies: embrace a growth mindset, practice mindfulness, and seek support.

Now let's discover the three P's, which will enable you to implement strategies for conquering procrastination and overcoming the four fears.

The Three P's

The three P's are *prepare*, *prioritize*, and *plan*. Let's start with *prepare*.

Prepare. Preparation is an important strategy for overcoming procrastination because it reduces the feeling of being overwhelmed and makes it easier to start working. Here are some ways to implement this strategy.

Instead of looking at a large task as one big, daunting task, break it down into smaller, more manageable steps. This makes it easier to focus on one step at a time and see progress along the way. Keep breaking down projects and tasks until you are left with manageable steps. This process may take several layers.

The next strategy is gathering. Gather necessary materials ahead of time. Make sure you have all the materials you need before starting a task: books, notes, equipment, supplies. Having everything you need on hand prevents delays and interruptions.

Identify and eliminate any distractions that prevent you from focusing on your work. This could include turning off your phone, closing unnecessary tabs on your computer, or finding a quiet place to work. If this is something you struggle with, we will discuss ideas on eliminating distractions later in this chapter.

Prioritize. Prioritizing ensures that important deadlines are met and prevents last-minute scrambling. Priorities are the things that are most important to you. Daily goals are the specific tasks or objectives that you aim to accomplish in a day. Your priorities may be long-term goals or values that you're working towards, such as getting a promotion at work, saving money, or maintaining good relationships with your friends, family, and coworkers. Daily goals, on the other hand, are the specific steps that you take each day to move closer to achieving your priorities. For example, a daily goal might be to spend thirty minutes working on a project for a promotion or to make a budget and stick to it. Setting and focusing on daily goals that align with your priorities can enable you to progress towards achieving what is most important to you. Here are some ways to implement this strategy.

Prioritize based on importance and deadline. Determine which tasks are most important and need to be completed first. Consider the deadlines for each. This helps you to focus on the most critical tasks first and ensures that important deadlines are met. A critical task is a task that is necessary for the success of a project or a goal. It is usually time-sensitive and may have a direct impact on the outcome of a project. Critical tasks often require a higher level of skill or expertise and may require more time and resources to complete.

On the other hand, random tasks are not necessary for the success of a project or goal. They tend to be less time-sensitive and may not have a direct impact on the outcome. Random tasks are generally less urgent and require less skill or expertise to complete. It is important to prioritize critical tasks to make sure that you complete them in a timely manner, while making time for random tasks as needed.

THE EISENHOWER MATRIX

Use a prioritization matrix. A prioritization matrix is a tool that helps you prioritize tasks based on their level of importance and urgency. By placing tasks in different quadrants, you can see which tasks need to be done first and which can be put off until later. There are different variations of these prioritization matrices, but a common one is the Eisenhower Matrix (see table). Inspired by the ideas of the late president Dwight D. Eisenhower, it separates tasks into four quadrants based on both importance and urgency. Let's review them now.

The Eisenhower Matrix

	Urgent	Not urgent
Important	1	2
Not important	3	4

1. *Urgent and important.* This is the upper left of the four quadrants. These tasks that need to be done immediately and are of high importance. They should be done first, as they have a high impact on a short deadline.

2. *Important but not urgent.* This is the upper right quadrant. These tasks are important but do not have a pressing deadline. They should be scheduled and completed as soon as possible, as they will have a high impact on your goals and objectives.

3. *Urgent but not important.* This is the lower left quadrant. These tasks are urgent but do not have a high level of impor-

tance. They should be evaluated and delegated or outsourced if possible.

4. *Not urgent and not important.* These tasks, on the lower right quadrant, are neither urgent nor important and can be eliminated or put off until later if possible.

To use a prioritization matrix, first write down all of your tasks on a list. Evaluate each task based on its level of importance and urgency. Place each task in the appropriate quadrant. Start working on the tasks in quadrant 1 first (urgent and important), then move on to quadrant 2 (important but not urgent), then 3 (urgent but not important), and 4 (neither important nor urgent). Review your progress and adjust your prioritization as needed.

The Eisenhower Matrix is a useful tool for identifying and prioritizing tasks, but it's not a one-size-fits-all solution. Review and adjust your priorities as you progress. Keep in mind the context of each task and adapt the matrix accordingly.

Critical tasks typically fall into the category of both urgent and important. These are both time-sensitive and necessary. They may also require a higher skill level. A common tendency is to gravitate to simpler, quick wins by completing less important tasks, because it feels good to check things off the list. Here are some suggestions to find a balance between the critical and the random tasks.

Prioritize with a tool like the matrix above. Ensure that critical tasks are given the highest priority. A task management system such as Trello or Asana can help you prioritize and organize your tasks, making it easier to see what needs to be done and when. You may have this type of system included in your calendar. Set aside dedicated blocks of time for working on critical tasks in order to focus on accomplishing them efficiently.

Take breaks: give yourself time to recharge. This enables you to stay focused and prevent burnout. Also, seek help when needed. If you are feeling overwhelmed, don't be afraid to ask for help: it's better to do that than to struggle on your own and risk missing deadlines or making mistakes. Always seek help instead of trying to strike out on your own when failure may be at hand.

The next step: eliminate low-priority tasks. Once you've identified tasks that are not important or that can be put off to later, consider eliminating them or delegating them if that's possible. This frees up time and energy for more important tasks. By using a prioritization matrix and eliminating low-priority items, you can ensure that important deadlines are met and prevent last-minute scrambling.

Plan. The third and final P is plan. Planning helps you overcome procrastination by keeping you on track and making it easier to see how much progress you're making. Here are some ways to implement this strategy.

> Plan out your day or week in advance by creating a schedule or a to-do list.

Plan out your day or week in advance by creating a schedule or a to-do list. It's generally best to plan out the entire week. Don't leave it to a day-to-day process. This will help to keep you on track and focused. It also makes it easier to identify and track the progress you are making. A great practice is to look back at the end of your day and celebrate everything that you have accomplished.

Set specific, measurable goals for each task and use them to guide your planning so you can focus on the most important aspects of the task and ensure that you are making progress.

Once you've broken down those large tasks into smaller, manageable chunks, be sure to schedule them into your plan. This makes it easier to focus on one step at a time and see the progress made on bigger projects. Use a calendar to schedule time for your task and deadlines so you can stay on track and avoid last-minute scrambling.

Creating an Efficient Workspace

Here are some general tips for designing an efficient workspace. Start by considering how you work best and what you need in your workspace to support your productivity. Do you need a quiet space to concentrate, or do you prefer a more collaborative environment?

Consider the size and layout of your workspace and how to use it most effectively. Pay attention to factors such as lighting, temperature, and comfort. Keep frequently used tools and supplies within easy reach, and use storage solutions such as bins, shelves, and drawers to maintain organization and reduce clutter. Add personal touches, such as plants, pictures, and decorations, to make your workspace feel more comfortable and inviting. Ensure the set up promotes good posture and prevents strain on your body, which may include using an ergonomic chair and placing your computer monitor at eye level. Many people have found standing desks to be very comfortable, improving efficiency.

Finally, be flexible. Be prepared to adjust your plan as necessary. Life happens, and things change. Be open to revising your plan if needed.

By creating a schedule or a to-do list, setting specific and realistic goals, scheduling smaller tasks using a calendar, planning your workspace, and being flexible, you can stay focused and on track and can see how much progress you are making. This can help overcome procrastination, making it easier to focus on tasks and work more efficiently and avoid last-minute scrambling.

Now let's consider how you can practice *productivity* (a fourth P) with three powerful productivity techniques. These methods and strategies help you manage your time, work more efficiently and effectively, and improve overall productivity.

These techniques include time management methods such as the Pomodoro technique, which breaks work into focused intervals separated by short breaks (see below), as well as methods for aligning work with your natural energy levels, such as ultradian work rhythms.

> **Consider using the Pomodoro technique, which breaks work into focused intervals separated by short breaks.**

The goal of productivity techniques is to achieve more in less time, reduce stress and burnout, and improve overall well-being. Adapt these techniques to fit individual needs in both personal and professional settings.

By breaking work into shorter intervals and aligning your work schedule with your natural energy levels, you can stay more focused and avoid distractions. Managing your workload effectively helps reduce stress and the risk of burnout, allowing you to get more done in less time. This also creates more opportunities for other activities and improves your work-life balance. Tools like DeskTime are used to identify work patterns and habits, enabling you to understand where you may be wasting time and how to improve your efficiency. Different techniques work better for different people so it's important to find the technique that fits with your specific needs.

The Pomodoro technique is a time management method developed by software engineer and life coach Francesco Cirillo in the late 1980s. It is based on the idea that frequent breaks can improve mental agility and that breaking work into shorter, more focused intervals helps you stay on task and avoid burnout. The name comes from *pomodoro*, which is Italian for *tomato*. The method is named after the tomato-shaped kitchen timer that Cirillo used when he developed the technique.

The basic structure of the Pomodoro technique is as follows: Decide on the task you want to accomplish. Set a timer for twenty-five minutes. This is considered one "Pomodoro." Work on the task until the timer rings. Take a short break. Five minutes is recommended. Repeat this process for four Pomodoros. Then take a longer break: fifteen to thirty minutes.

The Pomodoro technique is highly adaptable and allows you to adjust the time intervals to fit your needs. It's common to use shorter Pomodoros when working on difficult tasks and longer Pomodoros when working on more straightforward tasks.

A key element of the Pomodoro technique is using a timer to help you to stay focused and avoid distractions. When the timer goes off, it reminds you to take a break and recharge. While the Pomodoro technique is not a one-size-fits-all solution, and it may take some experimentation to find the time intervals that work best for you, it's a simple and effective way to boost your productivity and manage your time more effectively.

DeskTime is a productivity tracking software that allows you to monitor your work habits and identify areas where you can improve your productivity. Running in the background, it automatically tracks the time spent on different apps, websites, and documents, providing detailed reports on your work patterns. The Productivity Pulse feature displays your productivity levels in real time, allowing you to see how you're doing throughout the day. An ad blocking feature allows you to block distracting websites and apps, so that you stay focused and avoid procrastination. Reports and analytics provide insight into your work habits, including the amount of time you spend on different tasks, when you're most productive, and which apps and websites you use most. Integration with other productivity tools such as calendars and to-do lists provide a more holistic view of your work habits. A team management feature tracks the productivity of your team members and helps you implement a more organized workflow. This is a powerful tool for anyone looking to improve their productivity and better understand their work habits. By tracking your time and providing detailed reports, DeskTime helps you identify areas where you're wasting time and make changes to work more efficiently.

Ultradian work rhythms refer to natural fluctuations in energy and focus throughout the day. These rhythms can last anywhere from ninety minutes to several hours and can affect your productivity. Understanding your ultradian rhythms helps you plan your workday around your natural energy level.

> Ultradian rhythms are natural fluctuations in energy and focus throughout the day.

There are a few different ways to discover your ultradian work rhythm. Pay attention to your energy levels throughout the day. Notice when you feel the most alert and focused, and when you start to feel tired or restless. These natural fluctuations can give you a sense of your rhythms. Try working for ninety minutes, then take a twenty- to thirty-minute break. See how you feel after each session and adjust your schedule accordingly. Track your energy levels and work habits over a period of several days or even several weeks to identify patterns and understand your rhythms. Partnered with a productivity tracking tool like DeskTime can help you track your work patterns and identify your rhythms. Remember, everyone's rhythms are different, and they can change over time.

The best way to discover your own rhythms is to pay attention to your body and experiment with different work schedules. Reassess your patterns every three to six months to identify any changes and make adjustments as necessary.

Productivity techniques such as the Pomodoro technique and ultradian work rhythms are powerful tools for managing your time, working more efficiently and effectively, and minimizing procrastination. With your natural energy levels, you can stay more focused and avoid distractions. Tools like DeskTime can help you identify patterns of procrastination and understand your work habits, allowing you to make changes. Using productivity techniques can help you work more efficiently, manage your time better, and improve your overall well-being by minimizing procrastination.

Stress and Overwhelm

Procrastination can be caused by a variety of factors, including stress. Many people who feel overwhelmed or stressed tend to procrastinate as a way to cope with or avoid tasks. The procrastination provides a temporary sense of relief, but ultimately leads to increased stress and negative consequences.

Procrastination is generally not considered to be a healthy or adaptive way of managing stress. It is often seen as a maladaptive coping mechanism that leads to negative outcomes, such as reduced productivity, decreased performance, and guilt and self-doubt.

We've already discussed healthy and effective ways of managing stress: practicing mindfulness, taking breaks, setting realistic goals and priorities, and seeking support from others. These strategies help many to cope with stress and avoid procrastination.

Let's explore how to consistently implement beneficial strategies and techniques. Persistence means continuing to doing something despite obstacles or difficulties. It is the ability to persevere and not give up easily. By recognizing and addressing bad habits, eliminating distractions, and practicing self-care, we can minimize procrastination and enhance our mental endurance.

Mastering Bad Coping Habits

There are several strategies for spotting and stopping bad coping habits.

First, identify the root cause and lack of focus. Are you feeling overwhelmed by your workload, or are you struggling with low motivation or low energy? Once you have a better understanding of the root cause, you can develop strategies to address it.

Set clear, achievable goals to help you stay focused and motivated. When you have a clear sense of what you are working towards, it is easier to stay on track and avoid getting sidetracked by bad coping habits. Employ a structured schedule to help you stay organized and on track. This might involve setting aside specific times, not just for work, but for breaks and leisure activities. As we've already noted, it's important to take breaks to rest and recharge. Instead of relying on bad coping habits to deal with stress or boredom, try taking a walk, stretching, or engaging in a relaxing activity like meditation or yoga.

The second strategy for remaining persistent is to eliminate distractions. We've already discussed this topic, but let's dig a little deeper and explore specific tips to eliminate distractions.

Determine what types of interruptions are acceptable and when they are acceptable, then communicate these boundaries to your colleagues. If possible, create a separate workspace where you can focus without interruptions. If you work in a noisy environment, consider using noise-canceling headphones. When you need to focus on a specific task, turn off notifications on your computer and phone. You might also consider removing social media apps such as Facebook or Instagram from your phone to break the habit of checking these sites 24/7.

Consider using the Pomodoro technique to stay on track and avoid distractions. Again, it's important to take breaks to rest your mind and recharge. Breaks are essential to defeating procrastination.

The third and final strategy to remain persistent is self-care. Several self-care techniques can minimize procrastination, enhance focus, and maintain mental endurance and productivity. These techniques include: meditation to improve focus and concentration, and reduce stress; regular exercise, yoga, and healthy eating habits support focus, concentration, and overall well-being; adequate sleep is essential for mental and physical well-being, with a recommendation of seven to nine hours of sleep per night; and regular breaks throughout the day prevents burnout and maintains focus. Consider stepping away from your workspace to relax, walk or stretch. Whether you're in an office or working from home, regularly stepping away from your workspace is essential. Adding in relaxation techniques such as deep breathing, progressive muscle relaxation, and guided imagery also reduces stress and improves focus.

> Get seven to nine hours of sleep per night.

If you struggle to overcome bad coping habits, seek support from friends, family, or a mental health professional. In addition to support, they can provide encouragement and help with accountability necessary to make positive changes. If you continue having trouble staying focused at work due to distractions, consider speaking to your manager or human resources representative for additional support.

Procrastination and mental fatigue are common obstacles that can impede your productivity and overall well-being. Recognize and address bad habits, eliminate distractions, and practice self-care to minimize procrastination and enhance your mental endurance. By spotting and stopping bad habits such as procrastination, multitasking, and eliminating distractions, you can improve your ability to focus on the task at hand and persist towards your goals. Self-care techniques such as mindfulness, yoga and exercise, adequate sleep, eating a healthy diet, taking regular breaks, and practicing relaxation techniques can foster your mental and physical well-being. By implementing these strategies, you can improve your ability to focus, minimize procrastination, and enhance your mental endurance and productivity.

> **Key Points in This Chapter**
> 1. Causes of procrastination include lack of motivation, the perceived difficulty of a task, and distractions such as social media.
> 2. Learn effective time management to avoid procrastinating.
> 3. Procrastination can be intensified by stress, anxiety, and other mental health issues.
> 4. Four common workplace fears: fear of failure, fear of change, fear of the unknown, fear of conflict.
> 5. Learn and use time management techniques.
> 6. Eliminate workplace distractions.
> 7. The three P's: prepare, prioritize, plan.
> 8. Use a prioritization matrix to sort priorities.
> 9. Plan out your day or week by creating a schedule or a to-do list.
> 10. Create an efficient workspace.

FOUR

Mastering Negotiation

Although you may not master everything there is to know about bargaining and negotiating, it's important to recognize that we negotiate every day. Like selling and leadership, negotiation is not limited to the professional workplace. Mindful leaders also recognize that negotiation is an important life skill.

Each of us is naturally better at certain skills. Some are better at music; while others are naturally gifted at athletics; and still others are gifted at arts and crafts. Nevertheless, all these skills can be taught. The same is true for negotiation skills: they can be taught, and they can enable you to take your professional and personal life to a whole new level.

Negotiation, like other skills, is highly individualized. In this chapter, we'll explore ways for you to develop negotiation strategy that works for you.

Strengthening your negotiation abilities is essential for effectively navigating difficult situations, managing conflicts, and facilitating cooperation when bargaining with others.

Negotiation skills can help with day-to-day communication issues too.

Why not begin by resolving that from this point forward, you're never going to get the short end of the deal again?

To begin with, negotiation simply means to arrange for or bring an agreement about by discussion and settlement of terms. That means preparing for some give-and-take, with interaction going back and forth, ultimately ending up with a settlement of terms.

> You always want the other party on the other side to know you are willing to walk away at any time.

Let's start with one important point: you always want the other party on the other side to know you are willing to walk away at any time; that it's not that big a deal to you. You may be negotiating for something you really want, like a particular car or house, but you still give the impression that you can walk away at any point.

Do It Afraid

Some people experience a feeling of dread when they think about negotiating. They get a feeling in the pit of their stomach and begin thinking to themselves, "I don't know if I can do it." They may feel intimidated by the idea of negotiating. However, the truth is that negotiation is like any other skill: it can be learned and improved with practice.

Maybe you've heard this saying: "Do it afraid." When you walk in and act, even though you're afraid, and at the other end you end up thinking, "That wasn't as bad as I thought it would be." Maybe you realize that you can do it differently or foresee some undesired outcome next time.

"Doing it afraid" produces confidence. This is the key to enhancing your negotiating abilities: you just do it enough. As you go through negotiation after negotiation, your confidence builds. You become more comfortable with the process, and discover that it's not as bad as you thought it would be.

There are three critical factors in every negotiation: *knowledge*, *perspective*, and *flexibility*.

Three Critical Factors in Negotiation
1. Knowledge
2. Perspective
3. Flexibility

Knowledge: The Power of Preparation

There is a common proverb in the world of real estate. It says that in real estate, only three things matter: location, location, and location. In the arena of negotiating, it's preparation, preparation, preparation. That's the key to successful negotiating.

If you're well prepared, you will know all the options that are available to you. Knowing your options allows you to flex and adapt to whatever situation comes up. Whatever's thrown in front of you, you'll be able to respond in an appropriate way.

Knowledge is critical for negotiation, and preparation is critical for knowledge. Conduct research to learn about the person or organization that you're negotiating with. The more you can learn, the more flexible you're going to be, because knowledge is power.

Say you're buying a used car. You sit down with the couple who own it, you present your $7,000 offer, and you wait for them to explode with rage. Instead, the husband looks at his wife and says, "Well, what do you think, dear?" The wife says, "Oh, why don't we go ahead and take it and just get rid of the car?"

What is your first response when the other party says yes to your first offer? Very likely it will be, "I probably could have done better. Maybe I could have gotten it for $6,500 or $6,000." In fact, if you'd have taken them a $6,500 or $6,000 offer and they'd accepted it, you would have thought you could have done better. You see, it has nothing to do with the price. It has to do with the way people say yes to you.

What would your second response be if the seller jumped at an offer that you didn't expect them to take? Probably that there's something wrong with the car: "There's something wrong here that I didn't figure on."

Those two responses are extremely predictable. The lesson here is that certain predictable responses to the maneuvers take place in this process. Here is where preparation comes in.

If you can learn what these predictable responses are, when you make a proposition and the other party comes back with a predictable response, preparation enables us to know in advance how to deal with that response. In short, ensure we're prepared for predictable responses.

> Learn the predictable responses in negotiating.

Perspective

Another key factor in negotiating is that everyone has a unique personality style, and so do people with whom we'll be negotiating. Consequently, no two individuals going into the negotiation process look at the situation from the same perspective. People don't want the same thing. Whenever we're negotiating it's key to determine the intentions and desires of the other people involved in the process. In addition, it's important to know what you yourself want out of this deal.

Price is not the only issue: many other things go into the bargaining process. If you reduce negotiation down to price alone, somebody's going to win and somebody's going to lose. There is a style of negotiating that says that we should dominate the other person, outsmart them, and trick them into doing things that they wouldn't normally do. But this is far from ideal. Far more preferable is the win-win solution, whereby both parties win in the negotiation.

Win-win negotiations build long-term relationships. It will almost never betray you to look for long-term relationships. They are so important that sometimes it's best to lose on the front end in order to preserve the relationship. Why do stores have sales? They'll take a loss on one item, to get you into store then keep you coming back on a regular basis, sale or no sale. That's creating a relationship.

Negotiation can involve other factors as well: shipping costs, training, and warranties of varying length. Look at every element when negotiating price. You can even do this with retail purchases. Look for flaws or irregularities in the item you want to buy. If you find one, go to the clerk in the department and ask for a discount. Look for every option, every element, every component of the negotiating process and leverage it to your advantage.

> **Five Outcomes of Negotiation**
> 1. Conquest: I win, you lose.
> 2. Capitulation: you win, I lose.
> 3. Withdrawal.
> 4. Compromise.
> 5. Win-win.

Five Outcomes

There are five outcomes in negotiating.

1. **Conquest.** I win, you lose. This approach focuses on short-term relationships. If you are winning and the other party is losing in every exchange, don't be surprised if the other party doesn't want do business with or interact with you. (Remember, these are life skills.) Those who view negotiation as conquest have a short-term perspective.

2. **Capitulation.** I lose, you win. Research in personality profiling assessment has determined that 14 percent of the human race is basically aggressive: they're "I win–you lose." Conversely, 86 percent of the human race is passive: "I'm willing to lose in order for the other person to win." Capitulation is not necessarily wrong. It could be a good (or even necessary) strategy to use in certain situations. But be aware that you lose–they win.

3. **Withdrawal.** You simply pull out—meaning that neither party is going to get what they want. In sandlot baseball, sometimes one kid has the bat and ball. If at any point they want to leave and take their bat and ball with them, the game is over.

4. **Compromise.** This outcome often produces lose-lose scenarios. Both sides will compromise to the point where neither one of them gets what they're looking for. Compromise is not necessarily bad, but you do need to understand that if both you and the other party compromises too much, you're going to end up with a lose-lose scenario. Nobody wins in the long run.

5. **Win-win.** The fifth, and best, outcome is win-win, or collaboration. Most bargaining and negotiating professionals try to create win-win scenarios. This is long-term thinking. This is where you build trust. This leads people to come back for repeat orders. Often a customer goes back to the same vendor that they used previously. Why? Because there's a certain level of trust. They've created a win-win scenario.

These are the five outcomes of negotiating. Can both sides leave the bargaining table happy? As we can readily see, the answer to that is yes.

Flexibility: Achieving Win-Win Outcomes

To achieve win-win solutions, we need to go into the negotiation with the idea that it's basically a series of problem-solving conversations. It's not an event; it's a process.

Begin this process by putting the issues out on the table. Start with, "Here's what we want to accomplish." There's some interaction back and forth. "What's in it for you?" "Here's what it's in it for me; here's what I want to try to accomplish; here's what I propose." Then either you or the other person puts some kind of proposition on the table. At that point the negotiation begins.

Creativity is exceptionally valuable here. We need to be willing to think outside the box, as it's rarely just about price. Most negotiations, deals, or transactions involve many other elements, and preparation is key. The more knowledge we have, the more flexibility we have, and the more we're able to introduce new options into the process.

In Stephen R. Covey's *Seven Habits of Highly Effective People*, habit number two is "Begin with the end in mind." Great negotiators always begin with the end in mind. They know where they want to go: what they want to accomplish at the end of the negotiation. It's very important. Keep the end at the front of your mind throughout the entire process: what am I trying to achieve here? Consider writing down what you want to achieve on a piece of paper to take into the negotiation with you.

Here's why that's so critical. When you keep your end in mind and the other party throws an out-of-the-box option at you, you can take a moment and ask yourself, "Wait a minute. What am I trying to accomplish here? Is that going to accomplish what I've set my mind to get done here?" If not, you say, "No, thank you. I appreciate the option. It's a good thought, but that's not where we're going."

Keeping the end in mind also keeps you focused if somebody says something offensive, tries to get under your skin, or bullies or intimidates you. When you focus on what you want to accomplish with your negotiation, it better prepares you to adapt and respond in an appropriate way. This is absolutely critical.

Let's explore another tactic. Say you're a purchaser. You ask the seller for options. If you're at an impasse, you can say to them, "Help me out here. I'd like to do business with you." You could do the same as a seller: "I'd really like to sell this item to you. I'd like to do business with your organization. I'd like to have a long-term relationship with you."

As you can see, the negotiation process is the same whether you're the buyer or the seller. Looking at the situation and understanding both sides is another effective way to prepare for successful negotiations.

> **The negotiation process is the same whether you're looking at it from the buyer's side or from the seller's.**

In any event, you can ask the other party, "I want to do something that's going to be effective for everybody, but I need your help here. Do you have any options? Have you got anything that's going to help us here?"

Don't discount the technology at your fingertips to help you in certain situations. Pull up an app or conduct a search on the Internet from your mobile device or laptop to do some on the spot price comparison with what other organizations are selling a product for.

As mentioned earlier, you can look for flaws and shortcomings in the item you're purchasing, consider cutting back on or eliminating features, or maybe you decide that instead of having all the bells and whistles, you can say, "What if I were willing to give up this feature? Could we then get into the price range that I'm looking for?"

Quality or service issues are another point of negotiation. This is especially important if you're doing repeat buying. Say you're a purchasing agent, and there was a major flaw in the service from the organization you're negotiating with: they told you they were going to provide a twenty-four-hour response to any service issues that come up. But you experienced a breakdown with a piece of equipment, and it took that organization eighteen hours to get back to you. Technically they were within the twenty-four-hour range, but your production came to a halt because you had to wait eighteen hours before you got a response. That could be a point of negotiation for the next service contract with that organization. Keep in mind that quality, consistency, and service are elements in negotiation, especially if you're determined to create a long-term relationship.

In short, thinking outside the box provides you with more options. Be creative in your thinking.

BATNA

Something else you may see in the negotiating arena is the BATNA, which stands for *the best alternative to a negotiated agreement*. In some negotiation situations, you may find the process is not moving forward. Say you want to purchase coffee mugs and you are unable to come up with a win-win agreement with a vendor. Instead of buying custom-made, personalized mugs, ask the vendor, "Just give me a price on Styrofoam cups." In six months, you can review the idea of purchasing brand-new mugs, but for now, this is the best alternative to a negotiated agreement.

BATNA:
The Best Alternative To a Negotiated Agreement.

Another option is going with another vendor, and you might respond, "Thank you very much. I appreciate your time. I've been doing some competitive shopping, and I have another vendor able to provide me what I need at the price I'm looking for. So, I'm going to go with your competitor." That may be the best alternative to a negotiated agreement.

Gambits in Negotiating

Roger Dawson, in his book *The Secrets of Power Negotiating*, describes twenty-eight different negotiating gambits. In chess, *gambit* refers to a tactic designed to gain some kind of advantage—say sacrificing a pawn for a better position on the board. Here the term basically means *strategy* or even *ploy*. Dawson suggests we should learn as many of the negotiating gambits as we can, not necessarily because we want to use them, but because it gives us an advantage by knowing when they're being used against us.

As you practice and become better at negotiations, chances are you're going to end up with eight, nine, or ten different negotiating strategies in your negotiation playbook. As you continue to negotiate and gain more experience, you can expand your list up to all twenty-eight. The point is to start wherever you are now. Do it afraid.

Here are some important gambits.

1. **Don't set your anchor before you're ready.**

What does that mean? In negotiating circles, *anchor* refers to a price, offer, or some other proposal. Sometimes the seller sets the anchor, they'll set it first. Basically, you're setting a price. Let's walk through this example to see how this works.

> Don't set your anchor before you're ready.

Let's say you are negotiating a purchase. The seller says, "We're going to charge a $100 per unit for this item." You're thinking $50 is appropriate and satisfactory and the price point you're hoping to negotiate. The seller sets their anchor at $100 per unit, but you haven't set your anchor yet, even though $50 is in your mind.

In this gambit, you don't come back with a price. You say to the seller, "I've been doing competitive biddings. I know what we should be paying. And I can tell you, $100 per unit is nowhere close to where we're ready to go with this. Here's what I'm going to do. I'm going to give you twenty-four hours, and I'd like you to come back and resubmit your proposal to me at that time."

You haven't set your anchor yet. You're still thinking $50; the seller is at $100. They come back and respond with, "You know what? We've looked at it, and we can charge you $70 per unit."

You're still thinking that $70 is still too high. But you're thinking to yourself, "Let's get this thing going." You respond to the seller with, "I will give you $60 per unit." At this point, you've set your anchor.

Now here's why anchors are so important. Once the seller sets an anchor, the price will never go up. If you offered to sell an item for $100, you are not able to change your mind and say you're now charging $110. For the purchaser, once you set your anchor, the price will never go lower than your anchor. Once you've said you'll pay $60 for the unit, you can't come back later and say you'll only pay $50.

Whenever you set your anchor, you need to be ready to go with whatever you've put out on the table. But you want to stretch the process out as long as possible. The strategy is, "I want you to go back, sharpen your pencil, and come back to me with another proposal."

You do that as long as you possibly can. At this point, you have not set your anchor yet; in your mind, it's still at $50 per unit. Try to get the other party to come down as far as they possibly can before you set your anchor by putting a price out on the table.

2. "That's my best offer; take it or leave it."

People often use this gambit to intimidate you or try to speed up the negotiation process. Here's the good news: the other party may say, "OK, I'll take it." The bad news is that they may call your bluff and leave it. Avoid saying, "That's my best offer; take it or leave it," until you are truly ready to walk away from the negotiating table. If they walk away and you then say, "Whoa, whoa, wait! I'll tell you what. I just thought about something. Maybe we can work it out this way," trust has just gone out the window, because you really didn't mean what you said. "That's my best offer; take it or leave it" is a great strategy to use—but only when you're truly ready to use it.

3. "Let's split the difference."

This is another strategy you don't want to use unless you really are willing to do it. To go back to our scenario, the seller comes back with a counteroffer of $70 per unit. If you reply with an offer of $60, they'll say, "Let's just split the difference." When they say, "let's split the difference," they're basically saying, "We are willing to move our anchor to $65."

Here's the strategy. If that's not the deal you want, you might say, "Thank you very much. I'm glad that you're willing to go to $65 per unit, but I'm still at $60." The seller has said they are willing to go to $65, splitting the difference of $10. But you can negotiate a little better by saying, "No. Thank you very much for going to $65, but I'm still at $60." If the negotiation continues and you want to ask the seller to consider a different price point, you can counter with, "OK, I'll tell you what: let's split the difference, and I'll give you $62.50 per unit." You've gotten a better price by keeping your anchor firm. But you don't say, "Let's split the difference" until you're ready to.

4. The chip-away technique.

This occurs when an individual is trying to get more out of the deal after you've shaken hands. You see this with car dealerships all over the country. For example, the salesperson offers and you accept the price of the vehicle at $25,000. But when you're signing the final contract, the dealer pushes the agreement across the table with a $1,000 processing fee. You say, "Wait a minute! What is this processing fee?" They say, "Oh, everybody's doing it. It's just standard procedure."

> The chip-away technique: trying to get more out of you after you've shaken your hands.

The seller is taking what should be considered overhead to chip away at you. You agreed on $25,000 for the car. Now they're trying to get $26,000 out of you.

Don't use the chip-away technique but be aware when it's being used against you.

5. Position of higher authority.

When you go into a negotiating process, you let the other party know up front that whatever deal that you come up with, you need to run it by somebody else. That could be a higher authority, a colleague, a peer, a partner, even a spouse. If you are negotiating a house purchase, you could say at the outset, "I'm going to have to clear this with my spouse."

Most importantly, this gambit gives you an extra step in negotiating. Moreover, when you run a potential deal by this other person, more times than not they'll see things that you didn't see. This technique gives you an extra set of eyes and ears. It enables you to go back to the other party and say, "I know we shook hands on this deal here, but I ran this by my partner, and it turns out that we have some other things that we need to talk about here."

6. The set-aside technique.

This goes back to the 80/20 rule: 80 percent of whatever happens will be carried out by 20 percent of the individuals involved. For example, in a not-for-profit organization, 80 percent of the revenue comes from 20 percent of the supporters. Especially in a volunteer organization, 80 percent of the work will be done by 20 percent of the workers.

In negotiating, 80 percent of the negotiation is done in the last 20 percent of the time frame. This means that you want to set aside the biggest possible setbacks or detriments for the end. Frequently the other party will try to get you to negotiate those things right up front and as quickly as possible.

You reply, "No. I'll tell you what: that's the biggest part of this negotiation. Let's set that aside. Let's work on all the smaller stuff first. When we get to the last part, we'll address that big issue." Here's why, especially if you're purchasing: It's like football; the closer you get to the end zone, the more the other person is involved. This is especially true for a seller, the more they have invested, the hungrier they're going to get.

Have you ever heard the best time to buy a car is at the end of the month or the quarter or the year? Why is that? Because the dealer and the salespeople want to hit their sales goals. They want to hit their quota.

In short, the deals take place within the last 20 percent of the time frame. Using this technique, you set aside the biggest items that you need to negotiate until the end, because that's when there's the greatest pressure for compromise and concessions.

7. **The tradeoff principle.** Whenever you're negotiating, you want to make sure that if you give up something, you ask the other person for a concession as well, so it's equal.

> If you give up something, ask the other person for a concession as well.

Whenever we give something up, we're vulnerable. Ensure that if you give something up, you follow up and you ask that other person, "OK, I gave up *this*, now I want you to give *that* up." There needs to be an equal trade-off.

Mistakes in Negotiating

There are also several common mistakes that people make in negotiating. In every one of them, the mistake ultimately comes down to the fact that the individual lost track of what they were trying to accomplish. Remember what Stephen Covey said: begin with the end in mind. What are you trying to accomplish? When people forget about that, they start making mistakes.

We need to understand that we're trying to achieve an end. That may mean you may need to put your ego and self-esteem on the side. Sometimes it's simply a matter of bad chemistry between you and the other party. In some situations, negotiators realize they're not connecting with the other party, and they're wise enough to remove themselves from the equation. Then they introduce somebody else as a replacement in the negotiating process. Some organizations will put one person in for negotiating up to a certain point and then pull that person and bring somebody else in to complete it. It may be that the initial person is good at the beginning of the negotiation process but doesn't have the ability to take it to the end and consummate the agreement. Here the organization is trying to play on all their strengths and use every option available to them.

* * *

In conclusion, effective negotiating requires effort, thought, and intentional action. It isn't necessarily going to be easy, but it is certainly the case that when you become better at negotiating, you're going to be respected and even sought out. Mindful leaders use negotiation techniques in everyday situations, not just buying and selling. Enhance your negotiating ability and watch your career take off. You can control the direction you want it to go and may leapfrog others who have been in professional positions much longer than you. Why? Because negotiating is an everyday skill and many people are not comfortable or don't know how to negotiate in today's workplace and our society.

Key Points in This Chapter

1. Negotiation is not just for the professional arena. It is also a matter of life skills.
2. Preparation is the key to successful negotiating.
3. Strive for win-win solutions.
4. Begin with the end in mind.
5. The negotiation process is the same whether you're looking at it from the buyer's side or from the seller's.
6. Figure out where you want to go and try to move toward a win-win scenario.
7. BATNA: the best alternative to a negotiated agreement.
8. Familiarize yourself with some of the most common negotiating gambits and techniques.

9. The 80/20 rule: 80 percent of the negotiation is done in the last 20 percent of the time frame.
10. The tradeoff principle: if you give up something, ask the other person for a concession as well.
11. Most negotiating mistakes result from losing sight of the end in mind.

FIVE

Hiring: A Skill-Based Approach

The hiring process is one of the most important responsibilities a leader faces, especially when unemployment has been historically low or there appear to be few to no qualified applicants for the positions we're trying to fill. Mindful leaders are careful to focus on skills and employee potential rather than on gut feelings and biases. A skill-based approach focuses on hiring the best person for the role and considers how the candidate aligns with the team's needs and organization's culture.

How do you hire the best person for a job in your company? One major trend in recent years has been *skill-based hiring*. Here you focus less on a candidate's experience and education and more on skills and competencies.

> Skill-based hiring focuses less on experience and education than on skills and competencies.

Ninety-five percent of executives and HR professionals say that individuals with only skill-based credentials—earned outside of traditional pathways—perform as well or better than those with traditional degrees. In short, individuals with less formal education—such as an associate's degree or technical certification—perform as well as those individuals who followed the traditional path and earned a master's or bachelor's degree.

This research has been coming out to support this idea. Eighty-one percent of HR professionals agree that using skill-based hiring makes it easier for diverse candidates to attain employment. This opens an organization to additional avenues of employees. The more avenues to find qualified employees, the more choices we have available to find the right person for the position we're filling.

Traditionally, when hiring, the initial focus has been on the individual's experience. Do they have experience in running a kitchen? Do they have experience working in a corporate setting? Do they have experience managing a group of people? Next, the focus was on the candidate's degree. Does a candidate for a chef have a degree in culinary arts?

Traditional hiring practices place a great deal of trust in both in previous experience and formal credentials. The assumption is if the candidate has a certain type of experience or a certain degree, they'll have the skill set to do the job. But often this assumption turns out to be wrong. The individual may have the experience or the degree, but once you hire them and they are on board, they turn out not to have the skills expected or needed.

Traditional hiring may eliminate candidates that shouldn't be ruled out.

Because traditional hiring relies on résumés and credentials, it eliminates potential qualified candidates that shouldn't be ruled out. Moreover, traditional hiring depends upon subjective assessments. We may say to ourselves, "I'm not subjective," but in reality all of us are: we all bring our biases into work. When interviewing a candidate, we interview them from *our* point of view. While not intentional, it may not be the best thing because we may be governed by subjective impressions or reactions: "I didn't like the way they looked at me," or "I didn't like the way they pronounced a certain word." That fails to address how effective the individual will be in that role. Many interviewers work hard to go beyond their own biases, but still, some of that bias remains.

Consequently, traditional hiring can be a more biased approach than skill-based hiring. The traditional method involves longer hiring cycles: doing more interviews, more reference checks. All this is trying to remove subjectivity from the evaluation, but there's less actual focus on the skills that are needed to do the job.

Why do people excel at work? Here is one possible conclusion: individuals who are successful in the workplace consistently make the right behavioral decisions. They consistently make the right decisions in the moment, and that makes them successful in the workplace.

Four Questions

When it comes to thinking about how to get people to flourish in the workplace, there are four questions worth considering.

1. Do they have the knowledge to do the job well?
2. Can they carry out the necessary actions for the job?
3. What systems do we need to put in place for them to do their job well?
4. Do they have the energy?

As leaders, we're responsible for having the necessary resources or systems so employees can successfully accomplish their tasks. When we interview a candidate, we are trying to determine how motivated they are, because motivation influences their ability to do the job. But in skill-based hiring, the focus is on the skills and abilities to do the job well.

For example, let's look at what makes a chef successful. First is knowledge: they need to know about food and ingredients, how they mix, and how to cook them. They need to know about food production, especially if they're working in a big restaurant or institution. They need to know about production and processing. They need to think about what they are going to do in the morning and how that will affect them at lunch and dinner.

A chef also needs to be accountable for internal and external customer service. They're dealing with their customers, but they need the communication skills required to talk to sous-chefs, dishwashers, and the waitstaff. They need to have good communication and language skills, so they can express themselves.

What else does a chef need to fulfill their role? Culinary skills; food safety and hygiene; organizational skills; time management; effective communication; good judgment; self-assessment; and attention to detail; and physical stamina to stand for long periods of time.

At this point, we've departed from mere questions of experience and a good-looking résumé. We're concentrating on the actual skills needed to do the job. This is skill-based hiring. It focuses on specific skills and competencies needed for the role. We're going to define them: "These are the important skills needed by a candidate to be successful in this role. We'll use assessments and testing to find out whether a candidate actually has these skill sets. They will need to demonstrate on a skill test that have these skills necessary to fill this role."

> It's all about the ability to do the job.

In short, it's about the ability to do the job, not whether they have twenty years of experience or a culinary arts degree. This reduces some of the barriers we see in traditional hiring.

Benefits of Skill-Based Hiring

There are many benefits to skill-based hiring. In the first place, the focus is on objective skills versus subjective criteria. There's less opportunity for bias in the hiring process, because objective measurements eliminate some subjective bias in interviewing. By prioritizing their performance based on skills, you're looking at the candidate's performance and confirming that they can successfully do the job. You say, "Show me. You tell me you know how to do it. Show me how."

Skill-based hiring increases employee retention. When thinking about employee retention, instead of asking whether they stay in their *role* for a long time, shift the focus to determine whether they are a fit and they can grow and stay within your *organization* for a long time. This leads to better retention, preserving institutional knowledge, agility, and innovation.

With this process, the focus is on the skills needed for an individual to successfully do this job. But how do we get there? How do we bring skill-based hiring into our organization?

The Job Description

The process starts with crafting a well-defined job description.

A well-defined, well-written job description answers the following questions: First, what's the purpose of the job? Why does that job exist in your organization? You should be able to specify the goals of that job, why it exists, and what the organization needs the employee to do to be productive and successful in this position.

Craft a job description based on the purpose of the job and the skills and abilities needed to carry it out.

Next, identify the tasks and responsibilities required for the individual to fulfill and meet those goals. Define each task and write down all the responsibilities that the role requires. Then you go through your list and ask yourself, "To fill this responsibility, what knowledge do they need to have? What skills and abilities are required? What tools do they need to use?" Going back to the earlier example with the chef, they may need knife skills. They must know about stoves, ovens, refrigerators, and freezers. When you get to the interview process, that's when you can ask questions to determine if this individual has the required knowledge and skill set to use the equipment.

Then consider what the work context will be for this role. With a chef, evaluate where they will be working. Are they in a high-scale restaurant? Are they in an institution? Are they in a corporate cafeteria? All of these considerations may require different skills sets, so write those specifications down. It's important to have a clear understanding of what that job is to hire the best candidate and set them up for success.

Let's take another look at the example of a chef. Their purpose is to prepare, season, and cook dishes such as soups, meats, vegetables, or desserts. They're tasked with inspecting clean food preparation areas such as equipment, work surfaces, and serving areas to ensure safe and sanitary food handling.

Next, focus on the skills needed to carry out these tasks. For example your list may include the need to have coordination to do more than one thing at a time and demonstrate critical thinking to make the right decisions. Additional required skills may include the ability to speak, listen, and communicate well while also having skills in food production and customer service.

A potential Internet resource called O*Net Online offers an enormous number of job descriptions, some generic, some very detailed. Their list includes the purpose of the job, the tasks involved, the skills and knowledge required. The more specific you are with your search, the closer you'll get to a job description that fits your needs. You'll find some details in each description that don't apply to your situation, and you can easily eliminate those. But these descriptions provide a great starting place if you struggle with writing job descriptions.

Using all the information that you've assembled, create a job description for the position. Consider taking it to the supervisor hiring for the position or to HR and have them review it: "Here's what I came up with. What do you think? Is this true? Is this right?" Ask the supervisor or your HR contact to redline the description and make necessary changes. When you have it complete, use it in the hiring process. When you choose a candidate, ask them to sign the description, confirming that they understand the responsibilities of the position.

> ◇◇
> ## Job descriptions have to be consistently updated.
> ◇◇

Another important point: job descriptions need to be consistently updated. Managers, supervisors, and employees have a habit of changing job responsibilities and tasks based on what needs to be done to increase the organization's effectiveness. Consider bringing in an HR consultant or a similar expert to ensure that job descriptions are consistently updated.

The Job Posting

After creating the job description, it's time to create a skill-based job posting. Job postings are a mini–marketing campaign for your company providing potential candidates the opportunity to answer to the following questions: Why should I choose you? Why should I work for your organization? Build a job posting that attracts the right people for the position and your organization.

When creating the posting include the job context. What an accountant does in one organization may be totally different from what an account does in another organization. The work context creates very specific questions around skills and knowledge. For instance, you might say or your job posting might include, "We are looking for individuals who have excellent culinary skills and can prepare fried chicken." Or "We are looking for an individual who pays close attention to details and can differentiate between different culinary spices used in the Middle Eastern kitchen." Maybe that's the single most important skill for this job. That's totally different from saying, "I need someone who has gone to the Culinary Institute of America and has ten years' experience working with high-level chefs." You're asking for very specific skill sets.

Then you might end with, "We are looking for an individual with a high level of active listening skills who can handle many people talking to them at the same time." If you've ever been in a busy restaurant kitchen, you know that many things are going on: people are shouting and screaming. You want to make sure that they have those active listening skills.

Now you have a skill-based job posting. How do you start looking for people to fill it? You may post it on Monster, Indeed, or other online resources, but think about other alternatives as well. Talk to accredited training programs. Think about your job and what kind of training programs enables someone to be successful in this role. Maybe it's an HVAC technician; maybe it's a salon stylist. Seeking out those particular accreditations gives you more specific places to look instead of simply relying on candidates with bachelor's or master's degrees.

Go to networking events, talk to people, and say, "I have this skill that I need. I'm missing this skill. Do you know anybody that has it?" Maybe it's marketing, maybe it's branding, maybe it's computer skills or Excel. Someone might say, "Oh yeah, I know so-and-so does that really well."

> Get rid of help-wanted signs and replace them with skills-needed signs.

Get rid of help-wanted signs and replace them with skills-needed signs. "These are the skills we need. We are looking for an individual who has computer level skills," or "We're looking for an individual who communicates well with our customers."

Consider listing job postings with Craigslist or other nontraditional online sites as well as internal postings for veterans' groups, military spouses, older workers, disabled workers, even prison or work camps. Using internal postings can expose you to an entirely new set of job candidates.

One great advantage of skill-based hiring is that it knocks down many barriers that hold some people back from getting jobs. Some people don't go to college: there may be various reasons that make it impossible for them. However, these same individuals may be gaining skills either through experience, learning on their own, reading books, or other resources. The process described above allows you to find individuals who may be a perfect fit for your organization.

Interviewing

Now you've gotten the résumés, the applicants are coming in, and you're preparing to start interviewing. To keep the focus on skill-based methods, use behavioral and situational questions that relate to the skills and knowledge you need.

Let's look at an example. Say you're the owner of a CPA firm. You might ask a candidate, "Do you know Excel?" and the candidate replies, "Yeah, I know Excel." And that's it. But after hiring, you will realize what this person means by knowing Excel and what you meant are totally different things. In this instance, test the candidate's knowledge by asking very specific questions: "Tell me what a VLOOKUP is. Tell me how you create a pivot table." Then, take those questions and build tests around them.

> Find out whether a job candidate has skills that could be used elsewhere in the organization.

Another aspect to think about is organizational: are these individuals bringing skills that could be transferred to other roles within the organization? It's an added bonus if you're able to bring new hires into the organization for this job and can see them moving into other roles as well.

Use specific skill tests. Avoid creating tests that are three or four hours long; instead create skill-based tests that the candidate can complete in five, ten, fifteen, or even thirty minutes. Keep them relatively short and test only what you want them to demonstrate to prevent burning out the candidate.

Finally, make sure your skills test is not biased. The Equal Employment Opportunity Commission looks at discrimination in the workplace and find a great deal of bias happens in the hiring process. Ensure that whatever skill set you're focusing on doesn't have a bias in the testing phase.

When creating skills tests, it's important to get buy-in from the hiring manager. Ask, "What skills are relevant for this job? How do you think we should test them? How will we know that the candidate actually possesses the skill?" You may run into some hiring managers who reply, "I can just tell by talking to them." No, you can't. The candidate may have a great vocabulary; they may say all the right words; that doesn't mean they have those skills.

Here's a sample of a skills test for a chef.

> Please carefully follow the instructions. For each section of this test, you'll be evaluated based on your culinary skills, attention to detail, and adherence to the food safety guidelines.
>
> This is going to be a recipe execution. We want you to create a classic pasta dish: spaghetti Bolognese. The ingredients are ground beef, onions, garlic, tomatoes, pasta, herbs, and spices. Use the provided ingredients to prepare this dish.

Test the potential chef with something comparatively basic. You don't want to have them create a recipe for something that they may never have heard of. They may not know how to prepare duck à l'orange, but they may know how to prepare a duck or roast a chicken. Don't ask them to do something that's not relevant to your organization. If they're going to work in a corporate cafeteria, they're not going to be cooking duck à l'orange, but they may cook fried chicken, mashed potatoes, or spaghetti Bolognese. Make sure the test is relevant to the job.

Here's another example of a skills test for a veterinary technician: a dog has been brought in with signs of distress; conduct a thorough physical examination and record your findings. You may choose to bring in an animal and observe how they evaluate and diagnose the situation. Observe their approach and how they handle the procedure: are they good with the details? Are they getting the numbers right? Are they caring?

Here's another example of a test for a potential supervisor candidate. As part of the test, share information from a real-life situation in the day of a supervisor: "It's busy at lunch hour, the restaurant is short of staff, and orders are backing up. Outline your plan to manage that situation. How would you prioritize? What would be your resource allocation?" This kind of evaluation helps us understand how the candidate works and their thought process.

Active listening is an important skill for many jobs. Let's look at an example of this scenario created for a customer service representative: "Mr. Johnson is calling to report issues with their Internet connection. He mentions that this problem has been going on for a few days, causing disruption to his work. He is frustrated and wants a quick resolution. How would you handle that?" You can read this script to the candidate and see how much they pick up. Are they listening? Are they getting the important things right?

Selecting a Candidate

Now it's time to select someone to hire. Here it can be useful to create a scorecard to track the candidate's competency level. It could be a simple spreadsheet listing the competencies and skills necessary to do the job. Then you grade the candidate based on your objective test. Were they able to make spaghetti Bolognese? Were they able to get the dog's vital signs? This provides you with a much more objective view of the candidate.

You can even list qualities of your ideal candidate within the spreadsheet, stipulating what you expect from your ideal candidate and how each one stands up in comparison to it compared to other applicants. Also, go back and review interviewers' comments, and conduct reference and background checks if this is part of your organization's process. When reaching out to references, remember to ask them about the particular skills and knowledge required for a successful candidate. When talking to a reference, ask very specific skill-based questions: Do you think this individual can handle communicating out to many people at once via chat or email? Can you give me an example of where they did that? Again, you're looking for very specific skill sets.

Upskilling

Although we've primarily focused on external hiring, it's important to recognize that current employees may possess or be trained up with the skill sets we need.

> **Organizations that use upskilling are going to be much more successful than those that don't.**

In fact, organizations that use upskilling are going to be much more successful than those that don't. There are many benefits to upskilling. To begin with, it prioritizes performance. Instead of looking at experience and education, look at each individual to see how they're performing at a particular task that requires a particular skill.

In addition, upskilling improves employee retention, although of a different kind than is usually imagined. We want employees to stay in their jobs, but it's more important for employees to stay with the *company* for long periods of time. They are much more likely to stay if they have the opportunity to grow and build their skills. We can shift our mindset to focus on how we can improve employees' skills so they are motivated to stay and grow.

Improved employee retention also helps with a company's agility and innovation. Many companies monitor the market to determine where it's headed. If the market pivots or requires us to do something different, do we have the skill sets to make those changes? If we don't, do we have a program or a development plan to help our employees get into that place?

Versatility is also crucial. Wouldn't it be wonderful if we could take somebody who is in production and quickly move them into a sales role when the need shifts and we need more salespeople? What would it take to do that? Prepare our teams to be more versatile and agile so our workforce improves and grows as innovation comes along.

Often when employees are asked what they look for in organization, they say they want be able to grow. Upskilling—giving them the skill sets and abilities to do a different task or fulfill a different role—provides them with that opportunity.

Upskilling also assists with employee engagement. We can focus on helping employees be more engaged in the workplace and thinking about where their organization is going. If you're preparing for future eventualities and giving the employees the skill sets they will need, you avoid a rush for hiring people with the right skill sets. You already have the right environment, and you have employees willing to learn and grow. You're building a lifelong learning culture.

Improving Versatility

Let's now look at how skill-based hiring can improve versatility more specifically. Let's go back to the example of the chef and the skill set necessary to excel as a chef. What are they? Culinary skills, knowledge of food safety and sanitation, good communication, self-assessment, physical endurance, attention to detail, and active listening.

Let's focus on this last skill: we know that a particular chef is very good at active listening. Let's take that skill and consider what other positions require active listening. There's a long list: family therapists, social workers, clergy, audiologists, travel agents, analysts, public relations specialists, and supervisors. Our chef is a superior active listener and has good judgment and good communication traits as well—all of which a supervisor needs.

Can we move a chef outside the kitchen? Maybe we're seeking to fill another role that uses active listening. When you're looking at your staff this way, you're not limiting yourself to the fact that this employee is already in the culinary area and will be great as an executive chef.

What if you have a supervisor role in the warehouse that needs to be filled? You look at the chef and realize that they have all those skills as well. Maybe they would be interested in moving to warehouse supervision. Maybe there is a role in customer service that requires an active listener. With this outlook, we have the flexibility to start preparing people for other potential opportunities across the organization.

Let's start thinking about strategic planning. What do we want to do in the future? What action steps do we need to take to reach those goals? What tasks need to be accomplished? And what skills and knowledge are required to accomplish those tasks?

Next, we should map our talent needs. Once we understand our needs, both present and future, we look at the organization to see what we already have and what we need to develop through training and development to provide what we lack.

This ties into the future of the organization. As HR partners, we should work with our leaders to understand where they think the organization is going to be one, two, three, or five years from now. If the organization is going to be here, we must decide what talent, skills, and abilities we need.

Matching Skills with Goals

Let's see how this strategy would play out in an organization. Let's say the company wants to increase its market share by 10 percent. In order to do that, we need more customers, so we need a better database to increase awareness about the company. Next, we need to increase our involvement in our community. These are our two action plans to improve our market share by 10 percent.

Now that we have that action plan, what skills and knowledge do we need to develop in our team? One is data collection, so we want to make sure that our staff knows how to collect current or potential customer data. When our team is talking to people, do we have a plan for how they collect the data and do we know where to retrieve the data for future use?

We could consider creating a new software system and may need to train the staff on that system. Then we may want to look at sales. How do we encourage the staff to improve their selling skills so potential customers become actual customers? We may need to increase our sales staff or improve the skill set of our existing staff.

The above example includes the decision to increase our involvement in the community. That involves networking and branding, so we give our people opportunities to practice the skill sets of networking and branding.

As this comes together, we identify which skills are important to our strategic goal to determine the actions we need to take: here are the tasks and responsibilities the staff needs to fulfill, and here are the skills they need to accomplish those goals.

Now we go back and look at the job description. How will the job description change based on the actions we need to take? What skills and knowledge will that person need? Although these questions may relate to individuals, they also may relate to the organization as a whole. Perhaps everyone will need additional training on communication, or maybe we decide to roll out a new piece of equipment, a new tool, or a new software program for which we need to train everyone.

Surveying Employees

Now that we've determined our goals, the tasks needed to achieve those goals, and the skills needed to perform those tasks, we can evaluate our employees in light of these factors.

One way of doing this is to survey employees. You can send out a survey and ask questions like, "What are you really good at? What skills do you have?" You may also create a skills list and ask, "Here are some abilities that we're looking for. Rate yourself on these abilities."

Although this is an excellent step to take, it does raise a problem: not all of us are good at rating our skill levels. We may think, "I'm really good at this task" when we are nothing of the kind. Conversely, some individuals say, "I'm not really good at that," when they turn out to be the go-to person for that skill.

While surveys are imperfect tools, they are a good starting place, if only because it starts the conversation and motivates employees to think about their skills in light of the company's needs.

> For a more precise idea of employees' skills, we can turn to performance metrics.

Using performance metrics allows us to gain a more precise idea of employees' actual skills. When conducting annual performance reviews, we can ask, "Are we really capturing the type of skills that are needed? Are we evaluating those types of skills so they will take the company to where it needs to go?" We then ask these questions in relation to skills in which employees may be deficient or superior. We include all of these factors in that conversation.

These methods can all provide some extremely useful information, but the best measure of employee skills and deficiencies is to observe and shadow. People often don't like to take this approach, because it takes time, and sometimes we don't have that time.

If you can't do observation and shadowing, ask supervisors and managers to evaluate their employees in respect to knowledge and skill. You may ask a manager, "I want you to spend a couple hours with that person to see how they're doing and what they're working on. How's their data collection? How are their sales techniques?" If you (and they) can be honest and objective in capturing that information, you can start pulling it all together.

But it really does start with mindset. We need to be able to change employees' mindsets (and our own). It may not be relevant that the employee has been with the company for ten years. Are they good at task A? Are they good at B? Are they good at C? Do they have the skill sets that we're going to need in the future?

You can also use various platforms and professional companies to assess skill sets. Many of these come with an extra expense that you may have to budget for if you go that route.

More specific testing may be helpful as well. You may need people with skills in communication, management, or leadership, or you may need to have them proficient with Excel or Microsoft Word. You can test them to get a better idea and more objective idea of how they perform in these areas.

Certification programs are another option that can enhance the skills and knowledge of your existing team. Is an employee certified in a way that indicates they have that particular skill or talent? While you may look externally at certifications and licensing, don't overlook an opportunity to create internal certification programs which tie performance metrics to factors such as promotions, raises, and bonuses. We can say, "If you acquire these five particular skill sets, you're going to have a certain certification," and you can tie these certifications to raises. Again, we're talent mapping.

Finally, look at industrial benchmarks to determine what skill sets are required for particular roles. Many industries and associations will have that information and may include job descriptions with the skill sets needed. Even if you're in a large organization that is involved in many industries—

logistics, retail and merchandising, transportation—you can reach out to each of those industry groups and find out the skill sets and benchmarks for an employee in a given role.

Getting Where You Want to Go

With all this information, you can pull together a relatively clear picture of your current and future needs and how they relate to the skills and abilities of the employees you have now. Your next step is to figure out how you get from where you are now to where you want to go.

This consideration leads us to the learning process: the process we use to acquire new understanding, knowledge, behaviors, skills, values, attitudes, and preferences. Understanding how employees learn on the job is extremely helpful.

This process starts with exposure to new information and experiences. If you want to develop a certain skill in an employee—for example, leadership—consider letting them lead a project or a team for the day. If you want to expose someone to enhancing their communication skills, consider giving them a presentation at a staff meeting.

You can tie these skill developments to rewards. Reward employees for the precise skills that you want to develop in them for both present and future needs. Guide them where to place their attention when building their skill set.

Give employees time to process the knowledge and skills that you're developing in them. Taking time to build up skills and enable them to process new information is more important than learning quickly. It may also provide them with a chance for them to reflect.

Once the employee has started learning new skills, help them discover opportunities to practice the new skills so they become comfortable and confident using them. An outside coach or coworker serving as a mentor can give them feedback on how they're doing: "Hey, you're doing really great over here, but maybe you need a little work over there."

Furthermore, not everyone is going to pick up a skill set at the same rate. Some will take longer to go through this process. In order to get them where you want them, provide feedback so they can adjust and adapt. Even in today's over-hurried environment, provide them with the time to learn and grow. When they've mastered their skills, they can learn how to transfer their knowledge to coworkers. This creates a continuous learning environment, where everyone is helping everyone else attain new skills.

There are several approaches to skill development; shadowing by a mentor; role playing; giving the employee case studies. Workshops, seminars, e-learning, and online training and peer knowledge sharing are also great ways of acquiring new skills. Encourage individuals to share in a staff meeting: "This is what I've learned this month. Here's how I learned it." Create job aids and documentations that not only help your team do their job better but can also add to the learning opportunities. After a certain point, you may offer or have employees ask to explore advanced education.

Cross-Functional Training

Another important part of the picture is cross-functional training: training people in different parts of the organization, so they can see how their skills work in those areas. Define the purpose of the training and let the employees know that you're doing this to future-proof the organization.

Job rotation is another way to future-proof your organization. As you expand learning opportunities, you may have employees ask if they can test their leadership skills in practice. Rotating jobs or putting someone in a lead role on a project could provide that opportunity. The added benefit of job rotation is exposing team members to the work done by other departments and team members, which will provide a greater appreciation for what others do while sharing more about how the company works.

A valuable tool for developing management skills is Pryor+ online learning, which offers training in over twenty categories, including customer service, diversity, Excel, HR, leadership, project management, and QuickBooks. Other resources are over 5,000 online blended learning courses, over 3,500+ live virtual seminars, advanced administration features, and professional accreditations. These resources offer HR professionals and managers a range of development options for the organization's employees for continued growth.

Some recommended next actions:
1. Build a culture of continuous learning. Recognize and reward individuals for continuing to learn.
2. Get executives on board by determining what they really want for the present and future of the organization.
3. Work with hiring managers, possibly by creating beta programs which managers try in their departments for six months or a year.

4. Develop skill-based job descriptions for each one of your positions, including the skills that you and the hiring manager think are most important.
5. Invest in skill testing and learning platforms.
6. Bring skill-based hiring and upskilling into your workplace.

> ### Key Points in This Chapter
> 1. Skill-based hiring focuses less on experience and education than on skills and competencies.
> 2. Traditional hiring approaches may eliminate candidates that shouldn't be ruled out.
> 3. When hiring, rely as little as possible on subjective criteria and as much as possible on objective criteria.
> 4. Craft a job description based on the purpose of the job and the skills and abilities needed to carry it out.
> 5. Job descriptions have to be consistently updated.
> 6. Write job postings that focus on the skills needed.
> 7. Find out whether a job candidate has skills that could be used elsewhere in the organization.
> 8. Match specific skills with the company's goals.
> 9. Tie skill acquisition to rewards.
> 10. Upskilling is a great way to ensure a company's future.

SIX

How to Keep Your Best Employees

Today companies and leaders across the board are struggling with recruiting, hiring, and retaining talent. What factors are contributing to recent upheavals in the labor market such as the Great Resignation and quiet quitting?

The Great Resignation took place in the American workplace earlier this decade: according to the Bureau of Labor Statistics, some 47 million Americans quit their jobs in 2021.

Quiet quitting is a related trend. It doesn't mean an employee has left their job, but they have limited their tasks to those strictly within their job description to avoid working longer hours. Quiet-quitting employees want to do the bare minimum to get the job done and set clear boundaries to improve work-life balance. It is a way employees deal with burnout to help alleviate stress. It may also mean they are ready to change positions or are currently looking for another job.

To deal with such challenges, organizations need a strong, positive, and purposeful culture. Today's employees want a work environment in which they can feel comfortable and safe. They also desire caring and transparent leadership they can be proud of. Employees usually spend more time with their work families than with their families at home. They do not want to work for an organization that makes them feel they are on thin ice or that doesn't allow for proper work-life balance: this is especially true for generations X, Y, and Z.

Retaining top talent requires more than offering competitive salaries and perks. It requires a mindful approach to leadership that fosters a supportive and fulfilling work environment.

Here is a list of tips for retaining your best and brightest employees.

1. Identify attributes of high performers—your most knowledgeable and go-to employees, the knowledge bank of your organization.
2. Assess common issues with high performers. Employees want to feel valued and appreciated. They want to do what they do best every day. What does that mean to leadership?
3. Apply employees' strengths and knowledge to the work they do. When you don't allow them to do what they do best, it becomes destructive for the organization.
4. Create a sustainable culture for high performers. When it comes to employee retention, culture is ten times more important than compensation. If members of the organization do not feel comfortable in the environment, they are not likely to stay long.

5. Evaluate the culture from the employees' point of view. Leadership needs to be proactive in evaluating and driving cultural change.
6. Invest in employees in order to elevate the culture.
7. Create a confidential forum enabling employees to report workplace concerns along with their own wellness and financial challenges. It's important to provide a voice to employees.
8. Obtain information related to toxic leadership. Employees do not leave organizations; they leave leaders. An old saying, "The only safe ship in a storm is leadership."

> Employees do not leave organizations; they leave leaders.

Handling High Performers

Top performers outperform other employees by 400 percent. This number jumps to 800 percent when it comes to complex jobs that require a lot of information and interaction. These employees account for the greatest amount of organizational output. A high performer can boost a team's performance by 5–10 percent, so the departure of just one could lead to a significant decrease in productivity.

Companies that are skilled at identifying and engaging top talent perform better than those that aren't. Look at football teams: those with top-notch quarterbacks, great running backs, and superb offense and defense win the game for everyone. If you're losing your best employees, use their departure as a learning experience.

Discover the reasons your high performers quit. It is not every day that your organization finds a top performer, so it's a serious blow when they leave your organization.

Develop ways to keep high performers engaged in the workplace. Retaining high performers means instructing leaders on best practices for managing high performers. Stress flexibility, not micromanagement. No employee wants to be under a microscope.

> No employee wants to be under a microscope.

Give consistent, constructive feedback in a timely manner. One corporate leader gave this advice about timing constructive feedback: "Please do not go over five days unless you're dead in a coma or on vacation, because that feedback will lose value if you don't give it in a timely manner."

Give them what they need to succeed. Leaders use one-on-one time to learn how you can best support your high performing employees. Focus on learning about your employees' obstacles, resource needs, or changes that might affect their priorities so you can provide your high performers with what they need to be successful.

High performers can go rogue. They will often feel (or actually be) immune from the consequences of their actions, leaving other employees to blame. Rogue high performers feel that your policies and procedures do not apply to them, often because leadership allows them to break the rules, leading them to become difficult to work with. Determine how rogue high performers hurt your culture.

Implement your performance improvement plans for high performers and leaders. Organizations are not sued because they fail to follow state and federal employment laws; they're sued because the leaders do not consistently apply their own in-house policies about matters such as attendance, codes of conduct, dress code, and workplace harassment.

Identify attributes and common issues of high performers. Don't wait until the exit interview to ask the questions necessary to keep your high performers, such as, what type of feedback about your performance or recognition do you receive? What opportunities for self-improvement would you like to have that go beyond your current role? What kinds of flexibility would be helpful to you in balancing your work and home life?

What talents, interests, or skills do you have that we haven't made the most of?

Don't limit your high performers. Don't ignore them. Don't lean on them to do the worst jobs. Avoid burning them out.

Styles of Listening

To reiterate a point made in previous chapters, listening is the key to all employee engagement; it is the cornerstone of communication. See what type of listener you are:

A **comprehensive listener** goes beyond collecting information and understands and organizes it in a useful manner.

A **discerning listener** wants to gather specific information only.

An **empathetic listener** pays attention to the emotions of others and provides support and understanding.

An **evaluative listener** assesses information for the purpose of decision making.

A **selective listener** is biased, listening only to information that they want to hear.

A **silent listener** stays attentive but nonresponsive verbally.

Three Types of Employees

According to a 2019 study by *Forbes* magazine, you find three basic types of employees in any organization:
1. The freeloader
2. The worker
3. The entrepreneur

Freeloaders are also called *slackers*. Workers are also called *average employees*. Entrepreneurs are sometimes known as *exceptionals*.

Knowing the core personalities of these types is beneficial for helping you to lead, manage, and relate to employees effectively. This knowledge also assists HR in hiring the right person for the right job, devise better performance incentives, and develop more sensible career and improvement plans. In return, the organization benefits from better performance levels, a more synergistic culture, and more fluid organizational dynamics.

> **Three Types of Employees**
> 1. The Freeloader
> 2. The Worker
> 3. The Entrepreneur

Let's look at these types in more detail.

1. **The freeloader.** These employees, who may constitute 20 percent of your workforce, are looking for a source of income, not a job. They're only interested in getting the money they need now (although they are willing to work for it if they have to). They can be found at all levels in the organization, from the lowest hourly employee to the C-suite. Although you didn't hire freeloaders, something in your organization helped to create them.

2. **The worker.** These employees constitute perhaps 60 percent of your employees. They feel the need to be useful and would rather work for income than be paid for nothing. They have a sense of dignity, grounded in the desire to make an honest living and give a good example. They're productive and have a high sense of commitment and responsibility. They're your diamonds in the rough, your foundation.

3. **The entrepreneur.** This category can account for 20 percent of your workers. These employees have a high motivation that transcends the need for money. They are intrinsically tied to doing something that they love. They have a clear

vision and mission. They overcome the limitations of others, give their best, and will always go the extra mile.

Now which of these three types do you think the leadership in any organization focuses on the most? Results show that first they'll focus on the freeloader and then on the entrepreneur. The worker may feel overlooked. But remember they are your diamonds in the rough, so make a conscious effort to focus on and thank your workers.

Can you figure out what type of employee you are today and what type you have been in the past? Can you figure out your coworkers' employee types? What strategic and operational applications do you see for each? Because you have all three in your organization, each must have a strategic and operational application. What do you think each type thinks about their happiness, their success and legacy at work?

High performers focus on their goals. They apply the acronym SMART to their goals: they are *specific, measurable, achievable, relative,* and *time-bound*. These individuals evaluate their goals to see if they are appropriate and working for them. They also make needed revisions and reward themselves for achievement.

SMART Goals

Specific
Measurable
Achievable
Relative
Time-bound

High performers are hardworking. They put in the effort to stay at this level because they know the payoff seals their value for the company. They're organized. They plan their day and know how to find the tools needed to continue their performance. They are the librarians, holding the knowledge of your organization and knowing its history. High performers keep a positive demeanor. They know how to act differently from the way they feel. They are optimistic and encourage others. They show consistent effort and have strong skill sets. They often exceed their goals for time and quality. They fine-tune and hone their skills to stay in the work game. They embrace development and accept constructive feedback, because they know that feedback enables them to grow professionally. They want to run the next-level project or advance in leadership.

If you set up a training schedule, these individuals will respond, "I am there." Positive people get positive results. To recapitulate a point from chapter 1, they know that their emotional intelligence carries them further toward success than their IQ. They focus on personal competence, such as self-awareness and self-management, which helps them build their social competence, social awareness, and relationship management.

Entrepreneurial employees understand that 85 percent of your success and happiness is determined by the quality of the personal and business relationships you develop. Research confirms that strong relationships contribute to a long, healthy, and happy life.

A high performer acts like a leader. High performers know that leadership comes from anywhere and anyone in the organization. They are intrinsically motivated. They have found their *why*: their purpose in life. They lead purpose-driven lives, while creating a healthy work-life balance, minimizing work-related stress, and establishing a stable and sustainable way to work while maintaining their health and well-being.

Using these attributes in your hiring process, you can create interview questions around these attributes using the STAR model: *situations* or problems you faced, *tasks* you were involved in, *actions* you took to complete the task, and *results* or outcomes from your actions.

The STAR Model for Interviewing Questions

Situations   **T**asks   **A**ctions   **R**esults

An example of a STAR interview question: "Carolyn, tell me about a time where you displayed optimism and respect toward a difficult team member. How did you do this, and what positive results did you achieve?"

Take a look at the attributes of high performers. This is what you want in your organization, and to build your onboarding process around these attributes.

Despite their talents, high performers may have traits and habits that interfere with their success in the workplace. With good leadership, you're able to anticipate these issues and help high performers manage these common traits.

Employers tend to rely on high performers, who may feel intense pressure not to disappoint. But even high performers get burned out. Their desire to succeed can lead to overwork.

High performers can become easily bored. They may feel limited and constrained if they don't have the opportunity to grow, which causes them to feel unappreciated and disengaged at work.

Some high performers have trouble working as part of a team. They might get impatient with the output of other employees and believe they could do a better job working independently. They can become rogue high performers and may need to be reminded that patience is a virtue.

Why They Leave

A top executive in a major company said that one day she returned from lunch, and one of her top performers had left a sticky note on his computer monitor that read, "I quit."

Why do things like this happen? Why do the best and brightest leave you? Here are some reasons:

1. Money. Money isn't everything, but it's up there with oxygen.
2. They don't like their leaders and managers. Remember, employees don't leave organizations: they leave their leaders.
3. No opportunities for career development. They're just bored at work.
4. Too much stress and overwork, leading to burnout. Burnout affects us mentally, physically, emotionally, and spiritually.
5. A clash of cultures. The individual's culture clashes with that of the organization.

6. They don't feel appreciated. No one says please, thank you, or you're welcome.
7. Taking back control for themselves; they want to be empowered.

Measuring Organization Strength

Here are some sample employee questions to measure the strength of your organization's culture, taken from *First, Break All the Rules: What the World's Greatest Managers Do Differently* by Marcus Buckingham and Curt Coffman:

1. Do you know what's expected of you at work?
2. At work, do you have the opportunity to do what you do best every day?
3. Does your leader seem to care about you as a person?
4. At work, do your opinions seem to count?
5. This last year, have you had opportunities at work to learn and grow?

Questions like these can give powerful clues to the strengths and weaknesses of your company's culture. Some companies use these questions as part of their leadership merit reviews. It's all about the culture. Culture can eat strategy for breakfast.

Dealing with Rogues

As we've seen in countless spy thrillers, operatives can go rogue. This is as true in business organizations as in secret-agent circles.

High performers are typically employees that get things done, often delivering high-profile, last-minute material that is perceived as hugely valuable. They end up as the go-to people for the higher-ups.

The downside is that when high performers go rogue, they can wreak dramatic effects on your business and your staff. You can end up with *The Bourne Legacy* in your organization.

Rogue performers often create a "nobody else is good enough" bottleneck. As far as they are concerned, they are rock stars and have never needed support from others. In their minds, their entire career has been one success after another. Eventually this translates to an attitude that nobody else is worthy to work with them, so they have to do everything.

Rogue high performers have exacting standards that must be met: no codes go out without a 100 percent unit test coverage, and no design can be signed off on until they have been through it with a fine-tooth comb. Since they're the only ones doing the reviewing, their designs go out without review.

Rogue high performers are difficult to work with. They struggle to connect with lesser mortals, which makes working relationships difficult, because, as we've seen, nobody else is good enough. They tend to talk down to others, who resent being patronized by them. They can (and do) break the rules. They believe that when you are this good, you can behave how you like, because you get things done. They feel no need to treat people with courtesy or professionalism.

Rogue high performers cost money, especially in areas with intense competition for talent, such as marketing and sales. Other employees, fed up with the rogues, decide things will be better elsewhere and move on. Senior leadership typically rationalizes this away by saying, "The company is better off without them." In that case, why did you hire this worker in the first place and put them on key projects with rogue high performers? When you sacrifice other employees to preserve the ego of the rogue high performer, you have to hire new employees all the time. And having employees leave your organization costs you more than hiring employees.

High performers don't go rogue overnight. It tends to be a gradual process. They will insert themselves into critical paths of projects one at a time, and their behavior slowly gets worse. If this tendency isn't nipped in the bud, by the time everyone realizes what has been happening, this behavior has been normalized. Not rocking the boat becomes the default option, which allows the situation to escalate.

This trend now defines your culture. Suddenly you have a toxic culture. Rogue high performers are running the show, and morale is plummeting. The senior leadership doesn't know what to do; they have no ideas and have tried nothing. But the genie is out of the bottle. Rogue high performers see nothing wrong with how they work. Eventually, they even stop paying lip service to the higher-ups, as they know that no action will be taken. They are getting so much done that the company can't possibly run without them.

Dealing with Rogue Employees

Who are your high performers on your team? The individuals you can always count on to produce repeatedly. Who are the ones that are easy to manage, who understand what they need to do and get it done? It's time to fire them—at least from their current position, not from the organization.

Managers spend a lot of time and energy getting poor performers out of key positions when they should focus on transitioning high performers out of their current positions. All too often, managers take top performers for granted. Leaders know that one day, they will take their jobs. Until then, the leaders are happy to enjoy high performers' consistent results while the leaders themselves work on bigger problems.

Such a disposition towards high performers is a big problem. Top performers know they are top performers, and as much as they love to excel in their role, they are also acutely aware of their ability to do bigger, better things for more pay and power.

> Constant vigilance is needed to deal with rogue high performers.

Consequently, leaders need to stop these trends before they pick up momentum. Constant vigilance is needed to deal with rogue high performers. Listen to your employees when they report issues, and don't assume these workers are the problem, because things are getting done. Stop the signs early and shut down this behavior. In the long term, you'll be glad you did. According to research, average employees are afraid to go to managers and complain about rogue high performers because managers tend to put off their concerns because of the rogues' production levels. The managers leave it up to the worker—the average employee—to resolve their own conflict. But no one wants to work in a negative culture, so they end up leaving you.

Company Culture: A Sword and Shield

The best companies use culture as both a sword and a shield to improve performance and reduce risk. They highlight the cultural component in job listings, hiring, onboarding, and orientation. Highlight that you have a positive culture, and talk about the components that make up that culture, especially in job listings for open positions. Most importantly, superior organizations make culture a quantifiable part of performance evaluation for all employees.

Is it time to fire rogue high performers? Who are they? The individuals you can always count on to produce time and time again without any oversight. As with regular high performers, it's time to fire them—from their current position, not from the organization. You might not want to have them to be project managers or team leads. Managers spend a lot of time and energy getting poor performance out of key positions when we should focus on transitioning rogue high performers out of their current positions.

A rogue high performer who goes off script is a big problem. It doesn't matter how great an employee's numbers are: if they make all other employees miserable, if they constantly spread negativity or drag other employees down, it doesn't matter how exceptional they are on paper. If you have toxic employees in your organization, you have to apply your performance improvement plan with them as well.

This is the case for a couple of reasons. In a world where competitors are quick to copy product features, the speed of product output matters over everything else. If you have toxic employees within your organization, you'll have other employees who are scared to have meetings with them. Employees will be spending time on politics, walking on eggshells—What can I say? What can't I say? How should I act?—rather than carrying out their duties.

As we've repeatedly seen, emotional intelligence is much more important than technical skills or IQ. IQ measures your reasoning and problem-solving abilities, but it is not a guarantee of success. It doesn't measure your creativity, curiosity, or emotional readiness.

We're in an era where emotional intelligence is an increasingly important asset. Technical skills are being commoditized. The differentiator between the employees in the future will be how they are able to work with other employees and their level of EQ. Employees with high EQ are able to provide emotional support to several other employees in the organization.

We should not be in the "one, two, or three strikes, you're out" policy. This is not a baseball game. Leaders try to sit down with employees and give constructive feedback, whether positive or negative (remember, within five days). Break through to them and penetrate any lack of self-esteem or effects of negative upbringing. Leaders get employees to a place where they can perform well and get along with those they work with. In fact, 85–87 percent of their success will come from the ability to build relationships.

Keeping Employees Engaged

How do you keep high performance engagement in the workplace? In the first place, know your employees and genuinely care about them. One size does not fit all when it comes to creating a great place to work. But leaders who take the time to get to know their employees and treat them with respect and trust will find that employees enjoy working with them.

One approach is a process called *leading by walking around*. Although you might not be able to have contact with each and every one of your employees, in a five-day work week, you might drop by just to have a social, small-talk conversation, and that will help you to build trust.

> Provide employees with meaningful work.

Provide employees with meaningful work. Employees want to feel as if they have made a contribution that matters. Provide employees, especially high performers, with challenging work opportunities that are meaningful. Employees who are satisfied with the type of work they are assigned are more likely to stay with you. Develop and train employees, providing training opportunities for employees to improve their skills and education.

Especially for high performers, set up a training schedule and they'll tell you, "I'm there." High performers want to improve their skills and grow to the next level. Use training solutions that work for everyone by creating individual learning plans.

Empower and trust employees. Let your employees know you, trust them, and have confidence in their ability to make decisions and get work done. Give them the opportunity to take ownership. Competence, integrity, reliability and communication are critical to building trust.

Who said adults can't have fun at work?

Have some fun. Who said adults can't have fun at work? After all, adults are no more than babies with big bodies. We spend a lot of time at work: all employees, including your high performers, want to enjoy their workplace. Give your employees time to build camaraderie and get to know one another.

What type of activities do you have at work where you can have fun? Maybe bowling, potluck dinners, employee appreciation day; schedule fun in the workplace for all employees.

Building a High-Performing Staff

To effectively build a successful staff of high performers, leaders must be able to recognize them in the workplace. This enables them to find the best candidates for promotions and develop future leadership through focus, professional development, and mentorship.

Look for growth leaders when making business decisions. Identify high performers by looking for patterns of growth. Look at performance reviews for current employees and identify who has put in the initiative to grow in their position. Gauge their interests. High-performing employees pay attention to detail at work by communicating directly and promptly and actively looking to improve workplace processes.

Know who makes decisions in your organization. Being able to make informed choices is a sign that someone can assess a situation and trust their own judgment and expertise. Pay attention to who wraps up group discussions and leads conversations towards making decisions. Similarly, actively make note of employees suggesting new and innovative solutions to problems.

Even and especially in this era of exponential change, certain things cannot be automated: creativity, ethics, respect, imagination, intuition, emotions, wisdom, humility, and integrity. These characteristics are crucial to an organization's survival. Technology is only the *what*; humanity is the *why*. When organizations find their *why*, they find their purpose. Let's live and lead from here.

Key Points in This Chapter

1. Employees do not leave organizations; they leave leaders.
2. Stress flexibility, not micromanagement.
3. Be prompt when making constructive suggestions.
4. There are three types of employees: freeloaders, workers, entrepreneurs.
5. High performers can go rogue, refusing to work with others or making their lives miserable.
6. EQ will be the big determiner of career success in the future.
7. Lead by walking around and talking to employees individually.
8. Give employees time to build camaraderie and get to know one another.

www.ingramcontent.com/pod-product-compliance
Lightning Source LLC
Chambersburg PA
CBHW072208070526
44585CB00015B/1249